GRADE
3

CORE SKILLS

Reading
Comprehension

Martha K. Resnick
Carolyn J. Hyatt

STECK-VAUGHN
ELEMENTARY · SECONDARY · ADULT · LIBRARY

A Harcourt Company

www.svschoolsupply.com

About the Editor

Martha K. Resnick is an experienced elementary teacher, formerly a Reading Resource Teacher with the Baltimore City Schools. She has served as a cooperative practice teacher, training student teachers from many colleges. Mrs. Resnick received her master's degree in education at Loyola College.

Carolyn J. Hyatt has taught elementary, secondary, and adult education classes. She was formerly a Senior Teacher with the Baltimore City Schools. Mrs. Hyatt received her master's degree in education at Loyola College.

Acknowledgments

Designer: Rusty Kaim
Media Researcher: Sarah Fraser
Cover Design: Alexandra Corona
Interior Illustrations: David Cunningham, Sue Durban, Rosemarie Fox-Hicks, and Holly Cooper
Photography: Kenji Kerins and Rick Williams
Composition: The Clarinda Company

ISBN 0-7398-5731-2
Copyright © 2002 Harcourt Achieve Inc.

Dear Parent,

Welcome to the *Steck-Vaughn Core Skills: Reading Comprehension* series! You have selected a unique book that focuses on developing your child's comprehension skills, the reading and thinking processes associated with the printed word. Because this series was designed by experienced reading professionals, your child will have reading success as well as gain a firm understanding of the necessary skills outlined in national standards.

Reading should be a fun, relaxed activity for children. They should read stories that relate to or build on their own experiences. Vocabulary should be presented in a sequential and logical progression. The stories in this series build on these philosophies to insure your child's reading success. Other important features in this series that will further aid your child include:

- Short reading selections of interest to a young reader.

- Vocabulary introduced in context and repeated often.

- Comprehension skills applied in context to make the reading more relevant.

- Multiple choice exercises that develop skills for standardized test taking.

You may wish to have your child read the selections silently or orally, but you will find that sharing the stories and activities with your child will provide additional confidence and support to succeed. When learners experience success, learning becomes a continuous process moving them onward to higher achievements. Moreover, the more your child reads, the more proficient she or he will become.

Enjoy this special time with your child!

Sincerely,
The Educators and Staff of
Steck-Vaughn School Supply

P.S. You might also like to visit the Special Features section of our website at www.svschoolsupply.com for other fun activities and learning suggestions.

Contents

Correlation to Language Arts Content Standards

LANGUAGE ARTS SKILLS	PAGE
Comprehension	
Drawing Conclusions	115, 132, 133, 140, 144, 151
Facts and Inferences	8, 14, 19, 20, 25, 26, 27, 28, 29, 30, 33, 41, 43, 46, 47, 48, 57, 65, 66, 67, 74, 75, 82, 83, 93, 94, 95, 103, 104, 105, 111, 112, 113, 120, 121, 129, 130, 138, 139
Main Ideas and Topic Sentences	70, 71, 85, 131, 132, 133, 147, 148
Making Judgments	23, 41, 124, 125
Noting Details	79, 86, 88, 91, 101, 108, 131, 132, 133, 145
Perceiving Relationships	96, 105, 106
Predicting Outcomes	24, 40, 52
Reading in the Content Areas	122, 142, 143
Sentence Comprehension	53
Sequencing	77, 78, 90, 97, 98, 100, 101, 106, 107, 108, 150
Vocabulary	
Prefixes	69, 76
Synonyms	78
Word Meaning	9, 16, 21, 29, 49, 58, 68, 87, 89, 96, 117, 125, 133, 140
Words in Context	36, 39, 76, 109
Research and Study Skills	
Dictionary	34, 52
Following Directions	21, 22, 141, 152
Outlining	113, 114, 115, 116, 149
Parts of a Book	13, 15, 16, 17, 37, 38, 50, 51, 52, 146, 147
Writing Skills	
Paragraphs	68, 84, 86, 91, 101
Punctuation	10, 42
Sentences	59, 60, 61, 62, 63, 90, 99

Vocabulary

The stories are comprised of words carefully chosen from the Dolch Basic Sight Vocabulary and the Kucera-Francis word list. Words that appear most frequently in primary reading basal series were also used.

This vocabulary list does not include every word students are expected to read in the stories, but rather is a list of words that are introduced as new vocabulary and defined.

Story 1
cheeks
fatter
furry
mumps
paw
rest
stripes
thin
tired
wait

Story 2
cover
otter
page
slide
spill
title
umbrella
visit

Story 3
breakfast
burn
pack
push
ranger
slept
spark
stamp

Story 4
heavy
riding
shiny
shout
sing
skating
sled
steep

Story 5
club
crack
fishbowl
joke
paint
save
settling
video

Story 6
awful
boasted
bowl
busy
champion
equipment
helmet
hour
hurt
practice
protect
ramp
skateboard
stupid

Story 7
base
bouncing
clumsy
giggle
muscles
praise
relax
relay
seriously
usually

Story 8
appear
brought
enemies
hoof, hooves
lizard
protect
scarlet
skinny
sorry
taste

Story 9
brag
capture
dare
mighty
porcupine
protection
quills
sharp
touch

Story 10
camera
clever
diet
helicopter
octopus
ooze
plastic
scientist
tentacle

Story 11
captain
crowded
engine
huge
leap
mainsail
passenger
sailor
thick
travel

Story 12
crew
dawn
drift
several
stir
storm
sunrise
sunset

Story 13

dinosaur
eagle
human
mammoth
million
mushroom
roach
swamp
swift
tear
world

Story 14

break
bubble
evaporation
experiment
fact
interesting
magic
puddle
secret
soil
wind

Story 15

cave-in
country
discovery
explore
mind
pasture
promise
straight
tease
tunnel

Story 16

apartment
beam
case
collect
diamond
jewel
lemonade
stole
thermos

1 The children had been at the big park all morning and all afternoon with Mack's father. They had gone on many rides and had seen many funny things. The hot September sun had made them tired. Some children were resting. They were waiting for Mack's mother to pick them up at six o'clock.

2 Kate said, "Look at that strange little animal."

3 They saw a tiny brown animal with black and white stripes down its back. It had a furry tail. Its tail was thinner than a squirrel's tail.

4 "That's a chipmunk," said Sandy, who was the oldest child. "Stay very still."

5 "Yes," whispered Joe. "Chipmunks are afraid of people. Don't let it know we are here."

6 The children watched the tiny animal run along the ground. Then it sat up on its back legs. It put its front paws up to its mouth. The chipmunk did this many times.

7 "I see something very strange," whispered Beth. "See how the chipmunk's face has changed!"

8 "Its cheeks are getting fatter and fatter!" said Ted.

9 The tiny animal's cheeks were all puffed up. Every time the chipmunk's paws went to its face, its cheeks got larger.

10 "I know why," said Ted. "It must have the mumps!"

11 "Poor, sick little chipmunk!" said Della.

12 "That is not why its cheeks are getting fatter!" said Sandy.

Underline the right answer.

1. What is this story about?

   a. how an animal's cheeks looked larger

   b. the chipmunk's home

   c. rides the children went on at the park

2. Why do you think the chipmunk's cheeks looked larger?

   a. It had the mumps.

   b. It was holding food in its mouth.

   c. It was blowing up a balloon.

3. When was Mack's mother coming?

   a. at midnight   b. in the evening   c. at noon

4. How did the children feel after the day in the park?

   a. tired   b. smaller   c. furry

5. What do you think Mack's mother will do with the children?

   a. take them into the big park

   b. take them home

   c. help them catch the chipmunk

6. What did the children think was wrong with the chipmunk?

   a. It was hungry.

   b. It was not happy.

   c. It was sick.

7. What do we know about chipmunks?

   a. They have large noses.

   b. They have fur on them.

   c. They have feet like birds.

8. What is a good name for this story?

   a. Rides in the Park

   b. A Trip to the Zoo

   c. Watching the Chipmunk

B Detective Sharp Eye says, "You will need good eyes to know who is talking." Write the name next to the sentence.

1. Ann said, "A chipmunk has stripes." _____

2. "Della, what other tiny animal has stripes down its back?" asked Mack. _____

3. "That animal acts strange," whispered Mack. _____

4. "Stand still," said Joe, "because the chipmunk is afraid of us." _____

5. "Here comes the car now, Sandy," said Kate. _____

6. Now, look back at the story on page 7. Who is talking in paragraph ②? _____

7. Who is talking in paragraph ⑦? _____

8. Who is talking in paragraph ⑩? _____

9. Who is talking in paragraph ⑤? _____

10. Who is talking in paragraph ⑫? _____

11. Who is talking in paragraph ⑪? _____

C Draw lines to match these.

1. small animal with fur

2. talked very softly

3. sitting quietly

4. not as fat as

5. part of the face

6. thin lines of color

7. in need of rest

8. the first one born

9. different; not like others

strange

resting

furry

chipmunk

oldest

whispered

thinner

stripes

tired

cheek

D These marks " " are clues. They tell you what someone said. This mark " is just before the first word someone said. This mark " comes just after the last word someone said. Put a (circle) around any mark that is not in the right place in the sentences. One is done for you.

1. Joe ⁽ᵃ⁾ said, Chipmunks are afraid of people."

2. "Is the chipmunk here?" asked Mack's mother in the car.

3. "Yes," said Della. "Look at the " sick little animal.

4. "Oh!" It has the mumps, Ted," said Sandy.

E Put these marks " " in the right places in these sentences to show what is said. Then tell who is talking. If no one is talking, write <u>no one</u>.

1. Tomorrow I'm going to Bob's birthday party, said Joe.

   _____

2. Mack said, I'm going too. Let's get Bob something for his

   birthday. _____

3. I'm on my way to the store now, said Joe. Come with me.

   _____

4. Mack and Joe went to the toy store. They saw many toys to

   buy. They did not know what to get. _____

5. Then Joe saw a puzzle. He said, This is what I want to get for

   Bob. _____

6. I'll get this ant farm, said Mack, because Bob likes bugs.

   _____

7. But his grandmother won't let Bob keep bugs in the house,

   said Joe. _____

8. Bob likes to build things, said Mack. I'll get this race car and

   he can put it together. _____

10

F **Read the cartoons. What are they talking about? Then answer the questions. Write complete sentences for your answers.**

1. What made the chipmunk's cheeks so fat? _____

_____

2. Where did the chipmunk take the seeds? _____

_____

3. Why must the chipmunk store seeds? _____

_____

4. Why doesn't the robin store food for winter? _____

_____

5. Why didn't the chipmunk talk to the robin at first?

_____

6. What makes you think that this may not be a true story?

_____

_____

7. Where did the chipmunk carry the seeds? Underline the right answer.
   a. in its arms
   b. in its cheeks
   c. on its back
   d. in its chin

8. Where does the robin go for the winter? Underline the right answer.
   a. to sleep under the ground
   b. to a warm place
   c. into people's houses
   d. on an airplane

9. Why can't the chipmunk go south? Underline the right answer.
   a. It is too poor.
   b. It is too big.
   c. It gets lost.
   d. It has no wings.

When Leon played hide-and-seek with his friends, he always hid in places where no one would think of looking for him. Today he squeezed between two bushes near an open place under the back steps.

Ugh! He bumped into something sticky. It got all over his face, his hair, his hands. In the sticky goo were little dried dots of stuff.

What a surprise! It was a huge spider's web.

The other children never found Leon that day. He was back in his bedroom looking at the Table of Contents of a book. He was trying to find out what those ugly little dots of stuff were in the spider's web. He did not want something so awful on his face ever again.

Stories We Like

Table of Contents

Underline the right answer.

1. How many parts are in this book?

   a. one   b. three   c. two

2. What is the first part of the book about?

   a. people who live near us

   b. strange animals

   c. people who live far away

3. Which part has stories that will make us laugh?

   a. Part 1   b. Part 2   c. Part 3

4. On which page is there a story about otters at play?

   a. page 17   b. page 42   c. page 68

5. In which story do you think somebody got wet?

   a. The Man with Five Cats

   b. The Umbrella with a Hole in It

   c. The House Across the Street

6. Which story will be about an animal's fur?

   a. Worm Pie

   b. New Neighbors Next Door

   c. How the Tiger Got Its Stripes

7. Where in the book can we read about animals that are different?

   a. Part 3, page 60

   b. Part 2, page 27

   c. Part 1, page 5

8. What does the table of contents tell about each story?

   a. the page the story starts on

   b. the page the book ends on

   c. how many pictures are in the story

B Detective Sharp Eye wants to know, "Can you tell which story each picture came from?" Use the story titles on page 13. Write the story title under the picture. One is done for you.

1. **The Otters' Mud Slide**

2. _____

3. _____

4. _____

5. _____

6. _____

Draw lines to match these.

1. something to keep rain off us
2. person who helps us learn
3. the outside of a book
4. to go to someone's house
5. little animal with brown fur
6. list of stories inside a book
7. name of a story or book

visit

cover

umbrella

teacher

contents

title

neighbors

otter

D **In which story might this be found? Look back at the story titles in the table of contents on page 13. Write the right titles and page numbers below.**

1. An old house is across the street from ours. It has no windows. The door is falling off. No one lives there.

   _____ _____

2. The skunk turned around and banged its feet. A bad smell came out and made our eyes hurt. We ran away!

   _____ _____

3. A teddy bear comes to life when the family is asleep. One night Teddy spills some milk. The family finds out about Teddy.

   _____ _____

4. That is where a spider lives. And that is how a spider gets food to eat. The spider catches bugs in it.

   _____ _____

5. The apple pie was ready to eat. We started to cut into it. Something long and thin was wiggling in the pie.

   _____ _____

6. Dad went to the airport to pick up his mother. She was coming to stay with the family for a week.

   _____ _____

E Can you make a table of contents? Use these story titles. Put them in the right part of the book.

Story Titles

a. Across the Sea in Sailboats
b. Schools in the Old Days
c. The Long Walks
d. Cutting Wood for the Fire
e. How Children Helped at Home
f. How Horses Helped People
g. Building a Fireplace
h. Children's Games
i. Keeping the Campfire Going
j. Wagon Making
k. Toys of the Old Days

Table of Contents	PAGE
1. How They Went from Place to Place in the Old Days	4
_____	5
_____	12
_____	22
_____	30
2. How They Kept Warm in the Old Days	36
_____	47
_____	54
_____	61
3. Children in the Old Days	68
_____	69
_____	80
_____	88
_____	95

F **Something is strange about these pictures. <u>Underline</u> the sentence that tells what is strange about each picture.**

1.

a. The umbrella is in his hand.

b. The umbrella is under his feet.

2.

a. Tigers do not go to zoos to see the people.

b. People do not go to zoos to see the tigers.

3.

a. The chipmunk's nose is in the wrong place.

b. The chipmunk's tail is in the wrong place.

4.

a. Skunks do not have feet.

b. Skunks do not wear shoes.

5.

a. Worms cannot learn to read.

b. Glasses help worms read faster.

6.

a. People move into houses.

b. Houses cannot move.

Ranger Smith said, "There has been little rain this year. The trees and grass are very dry."

"Yes, everyone must be more careful in the woods now," said Ranger Reed. "After you finish with your campfire, put it out."

"Put water on the fire," said Ranger Smith. "Stamp on it. Put sand on it. Push the wood around."

"Never leave a fire until all the sparks are put out," said Ranger Reed.

Then the rangers told us about two different families.

Ranger Smith said, "The Peach family was camping out in the woods in June. They slept each night in sleeping bags in their tents. On their last morning here, they cooked breakfast over a fire."

"Then they packed all their things. Mrs. Peach put water on their fire to put it out. Mr. Peach stamped on it. They waited until no fire was left. Then the Peach family got into their car."

Ⓐ Underline the right answer.

1. What do you think the Peach family will do next?

   a. They will run the car over the fire.

   b. They will drive away.

   c. They will call the fire fighters.

2. Where do you think the Peach family will go next?

   a. home

   b. back into the tent

   c. to visit a neighbor

3. What did they cook over the fire on the last day?

   a. dinner   b. supper   c. breakfast

4. When did the Peach family go camping?

   a. July   b. June   c. January

5. Why do you think they used tents?

   a. to keep the fire burning

   b. to keep warm and dry

   c. to stop the fire from burning

   Then Ranger Reed said, "The Stone family was in the woods, too. They were not careful. They made a campfire. When they were ready to leave, they did not put water on the fire. They just left the fire burning. They got in their car and went on down the road."

6. What do you think could happen next?

   a. The family could get a new car.

   b. The fire could keep on burning.

   c. The rain could put the fire out fast.

7. Why is it a bad idea to leave a fire burning?

   a. The food will not be good.

   b. The woods may catch on fire.

   c. The next campers won't want your fire.

8. What is a good title for this story?

   a. How To Put Out Fires

   b. How To Build a Fire

   c. How To Be a Ranger

B **Pick the word from the box that means the same thing. Write the words on the lines.**

burning	camping	careful
finish	ranger	slept
sparks	stamp	tent

1. someone whose job is taking care of the woods— _____

2. on fire— _____

3. to hit your feet down on something— _____

4. sleeping and eating in the woods— _____

5. come to the end— _____

6. small bits of fire— _____

7. a place to sleep outdoors— _____

8. trying to be safe— _____

C **Read the story below. Find the safe way out of the picnic grounds.**

The town of Butterfield was having its Fourth of July picnic. Many people were there when a fire started. Very quickly, fire was all around the picnic grounds. Five roads went out of the picnic grounds. Four roads were not safe, because the fire had reached them. Only one safe way was left.

The fire fighters told people to go out this way. People who listened were safe. Can you get out by doing what the fire fighters said to do? Draw a line on the map on page 22 to show the safe way out of the picnic grounds.

1. First, take the road that goes under the bridge.
2. Next, go past the outdoor cooking grills.
3. Then go by the big flower garden.
4. Then go past the swimming pool to the playground.
5. Go through the playground to the ball field.
6. Go by the ball field.

7. Now you must go across the brook to a big white house.
   The fire cannot reach here. You are safe!

fire

bridge

grills

picnic
grounds

flower
garden

pool

ball field

brook

house

D Are you careful to do things the safe way? Read each pair of sentences. Put **S** by the safe way. Put **NS** by the way that is not safe.

_____ 1. If the light is red, hurry across the street on your bike.

_____ 2. If the light is red, wait for a green light before you go across on your bike.

_____ 3. Don't run in the halls at school. You may fall or run into someone.

_____ 4. Run in the halls and you will get to your room faster.

_____ 5. Never put toys on steps. Someone may fall on them.

_____ 6. Put toys on the bottom step. They will not be in anyone's way.

_____ 7. The best way to learn to swim is to jump into deep water. The water will hold you up.

_____ 8. Don't go into deep water if you cannot swim. Have someone with you when you swim.

_____ 9. When you ride in a car, don't put your arm too far out the window.

_____10. Never put your arms out of car or bus windows.

_____11. When the fire bell rings, get in line as fast as you can. But clean your desk off first.

_____12. When the fire bell rings, walk into line as fast as you can. Look at the teacher and do what you are told.

_____13. If a bee comes near you, hit it fast with a book.

_____14. If a bee comes near you, stand still. Don't move fast. The bee will go away.

Detective Sharp Eye says, "Look at the pictures. What do you think will happen next? (Circle) **the right sentence."**

1.
   a. A car may hit her.
   b. She will win the race.
   c. A dog will run after the car.

2.
   a. The animals will help put out the fire.
   b. The animals will run away.
   c. The animals will drive off in their cars.

3.
   a. He will fall and get hurt.
   b. He will get clean this way.
   c. He will get on a bus.

4.
   a. She will call the fire fighters.
   b. She will change the tire.
   c. She will get a new car.

5.
   a. The clothes will get burned.
   b. He will put on the clothes.
   c. The clothes will get clean.

6.
   a. Someone will take a bath.
   b. The clothes will be washed.
   c. The floor will soon be wet.

It was not warm outdoors. All the trees were brown and gray, because they had no leaves on them. The children moved fast on the ice. What fun they had!

 After you read each part of the story, <u>underline</u> the right answer to each question.

1. What time of year do you think it is?

   a. summer   b. spring   c. winter

2. What month might it be?

   a. May   b. August   c. January

3. What do you think the children are doing?

   a. swimming   b. ice skating   c. dancing

4. What do we know about the ice?

   a. It is hard and cold.

   b. It is soft and wet.

   c. It is warm and soft.

5. Why do you think the trees have no leaves?

   a. It is summer.

   b. It is too cold for leaves to grow.

   c. Bugs ate all the leaves.

   Nearby, a steep hill was covered with deep snow. There was some light from the moon. Children rode down the hill and shouted to each other. Then they walked back up the hill, singing and laughing.

6. What time of day do you think it was?

   a. noon   b. night   c. morning

7. What do you think the children were riding?

   a. bikes   b. horses   c. sleds

8. How do you think the children feel?

   a. hurt   b. happy   c. hungry

9. What do you think it is like outdoors?

   a. cold   b. warm   c. hot

10. Why are the children walking back up the hill?

    a. The horses can't go up the steep hill.

    b. They can sing better when they walk.

    c. Sleds cannot ride up the hill.

   All the children on the snowy hill had on heavy clothes and boots. Some children wore gloves and others wore mittens. They wore heavy caps and earmuffs to keep their ears warm. A heavy scarf was around each child's neck. All the children's noses were red and shiny.

11. What did the children have on?

    a. warm clothes   b. sun hats   c. umbrellas

12. Jack's sled was going down the steep hill. When did the sled get to the middle of the hill?

    a. before it got to the bottom

    b. before it got to the top

    c. after it got to the bottom

13. Why were the children's noses red and shiny?

    a. They had used red paint.

    b. They had been eating red berries.

    c. It was very cold outdoors.

14. Where did they wear gloves and mittens?

    a. on their ears

    b. on their feet

    c. on their hands

1. Which of these do you think Sam will say? Write it in the right place in the cartoon.
   a. "Nice jump, cat!"
   b. "Bad cat! We can't eat pie today!"
   c. "Bad cat! I'll have to show you how to jump better."

2. Draw lines to match the answers to the questions.

   a. Why did the cat jump?

   b. What will Sam have to do next?

   c. Who was at the door?

   eat the pie
   throw the pie away
   Grandmother
   eat the cat
   to get down to the floor

1. Which of these do you think Mother will say? Write it in the right place in the cartoon.
   a. "A whale sprayed water on our house."
   b. "The sky fell on us."
   c. "There is a big hole here."

2. Draw lines to match the answers to the questions.

   a. Why did the water come in?   the next time it rains

   b. When will water come into   when the sun shines
      the house again?
                                           fix the hole

   c. What must the people do   A hole was in the floor.
      now?
                                           A hole was in the roof.

Draw lines to match these.

1. moving on ice   heavy

2. something we ride on snow   mittens

3. how a high hill may be   shouted

4. thick   sled

5. yelled   skating

6. gloves without places
   for each finger   steep

                          winter

E **Detective Sharp Eye says, "What can you learn from these stories? <u>Underline</u> the answer to each question."**

    The farmer had many chickens in the hen house. One hen was sitting on her nest. Six eggs were in the nest. Soon four baby chicks came out of four of the eggs.

1. What do we know about the farmer's chickens now?

  a. He does not have as many chickens now.

  b. He has more chickens now.

  c. He has the same number of chickens now.

2. How many eggs did not hatch?

  a. two   b. six   c. five

    Five children were drinking milk. Fran put a lot of ice in her milk. The other children did not want ice.

3. What do we know about Fran?

  a. She likes hot milk.

  b. She likes warm milk.

  c. She likes very cold milk.

4. How many children did not want ice in their milk?

  a. three   b. four   c. two

Two children were going to the store to buy paint sets. Lee had eight dollars. Lisa had six dollars. The paint sets were $7.85 each.

5. What do we know about the girls?

   a. Lisa got a paint set.

   b. Lee got a paint set.

   c. Lisa and Lee got paint sets.

6. What do we know about the money?

   a. Both girls must get more money.

   b. Lee must get more money.

   c. Lisa must get more money.

7. What will happen after Lee buys the paint set?

   a. She will get change from her eight dollars.

   b. She will not get any change back.

   c. She will give the store nine dollars.

8. Who had less money?

   a. Lisa   b. Lee   c. Less

The days were getting colder. Tim went to get his old jacket. He tried to put it on. He could not wear it because it did not fit him now.

Dad said, "We will have to buy you a new jacket for the fall." Dad took Tim to the store. Now Tim has a new jacket that fits him.

9. What do we know about Tim's old jacket?

   a. It was too large for Tim.

   b. It fit Tim.

   c. It was too small for Tim.

10. What time of year did Tim need a new jacket?

   a. spring   b. fall   c. summer

Donna and her friends had a club. The children met every Thursday to read detective stories. The detective club was saving money to buy a new video detective game.

One Thursday afternoon, the club met at Ellen's house. The children put their money together on top of a table.

All at once Ralph said, "Look at your baby brother, Ellen!"

The baby was painting the walls and a chair with Ellen's paints.

"Stop, Bert!" shouted Ellen. "Bert has just learned how to climb out of bed by himself. Now he gets into everything!" Ellen picked Bert up.

Liz said, "I'll hold him."

"I'll put all the money away," said Donna, "so Bert can't grab it!"

Ellen gave Donna a big red wooden box for the money. Just then Bert pulled away from Liz. He bumped into the fishbowl. Water, bits of glass, and fish fell all over the floor. Then Bert grabbed the money from the table.

Donna took the money away from Bert. Then she ran into the kitchen with the box and the money. She opened the big box. Inside was a smaller box. Donna opened it. Inside that one was a very small box. Donna put the money in it.

As she was putting the boxes back together, the middle one fell. The lid got a crack in it. Donna hid the boxes in the kitchen.

Ralph was settling Bert in his bed for a nap. Ellen was cleaning off the paint. Mark was sweeping up glass. Liz was putting the goldfish into a glass of water.

"Where is the money now?" asked Ellen.

Donna went into the kitchen to open the boxes. The money was gone.

"Who took the money?" Donna asked her friends. "It was right inside here!" She showed them the big box.

Ralph said, "Was it? Maybe you put it in the middle box, the one with the crack in the lid."

"Be like Detective Sharp Eye, Donna," said Liz.

"Let's see if you can find out who took it!" said Mark.

Then Donna knew. Her detective friends were playing a joke. They were trying to find out how good a detective she was.

Donna thought. At last, she said, "It can't be Ellen. She has paint on her hands. There is no paint on the box."

Donna said, "Mark cleaned up the wet bits of glass. Liz picked up the wet goldfish. But this box is dry. So we know they did not put their wet hands on the box."

"That leaves you, Ralph," said Donna. "Give me the money, please."

"I didn't take it," whispered Ralph. "Little Bert did."

"No, he didn't!" yelled Donna. "I knew you did it as soon as you said the middle box had a crack in it. I had just dropped it. No one but the person who took the money and I knew about the crack. I kept that middle box hidden in the big box to trap you!"

"Well, Donna, you've learned a lot from Detective Sharp Eye!" said all the children.

A <u>Underline</u> the right answer.

1. What is a good name for this story?

   a. The Pretty Boxes

   b. Donna, a Good Detective

   c. Bert Learns To Paint

2. Why did someone take the money?

   a. to buy a paint set

   b. to buy more goldfish

   c. to see if Donna could think like a detective

3. When was the money taken?

   a. when the children were cleaning up

   b. before Bert made a mess

   c. when Donna was in the kitchen

4. How did Donna know who took the money?

   a. Liz told Donna who took the money.

   b. The child told about the crack in the middle box.

   c. Bert saw the child hide the money.

5. What was the story mostly about?

   a. a video game

   b. a baby who got into everything

   c. someone who could think like a detective

6. How did Donna know who had not taken the money?

   a. The boxes had paint on them.

   b. The boxes were wet.

   c. The boxes were clean and dry.

7. What was Ralph doing when Donna hid the money?

   a. putting goldfish in a glass

   b. sweeping glass bits

   c. putting the baby in his bed

B A dictionary tells what words mean. The words in a dictionary are in ABC order. This is called alphabetical order. Look at the picture dictionary. Answer the questions.

Animals

donkey   A donkey helps people work.

hippopotamus   A hippopotamus eats water plants.

eagle   An eagle is a large and strong animal.

kangaroo   A kangaroo hops.

1. Which animal has feathers? Write the word. _____

2. If the word **lizard** were on this page, where would it be found? Underline the right answer.

   a. before **donkey**

   b. between **hippopotamus** and **kangaroo**

   c. after **kangaroo**

3. If the word **camel** were on this page, where would it be found? Underline the right answer.

   a. before **donkey**

   b. after **eagle**

   c. between **donkey** and **eagle**

1. What were Ralph and Ellen doing? _____

_____

2. How long had the children worked on the puzzle? _____

_____

3. Why did Ellen and Ralph go out of the room? _____

_____

4. What will Mom do? _____

_____

5. What do you think Baby Bert is saying in the last picture? Write what you think he said. Put it in the cartoon too.

_____

_____

D **Write the word that goes in each sentence. Use the words below.**

club	video	sweeps	save
cleaned	cracked	shouted	

1. He _____ the floor to clean it.

2. The kitchen needs to be _____ .

3. The _____ meets every Friday.

4. A _____ game can be played on a TV screen.

5. Why don't you _____ your money until you need it?

6. When the egg fell on the floor, it _____ .

Use this table of contents to answer the questions below.

Table of Contents

1. What is the book all about? _____

2. Name four places where nests are found.

_____ _____ _____ _____

3. Write the page numbers where you can find out about these.

_____ a. a robin's nest in a tree

_____ b. where a turkey builds a nest

_____ c. nests near water

_____ d. two places where insects build nests

_____ e. where a chicken lays eggs

_____ f. where duck eggs can be found

4. What kinds of nests are in this book? Circle the answer.

   a. nests of snakes   b. nests of frogs and tadpoles

   c. nests of birds and insects   d. nests of fish

B These pictures belong in the book about nests. Use the table of contents on page 37 to tell in which part of the book you would find each picture. Write **Part 1, Part 2, Part 3,** or **Part 4.**

1. _____

2. _____

3. _____

4. _____

5. _____

6. _____

C (Circle) the right word to end the sentence.

1. If it is a skunk, it has (sparks, stripes, spots).

2. If a flower has colored dots, it has (sparks, stripes, spots).

3. If the otter is warm, it has (for, fire, fur).

4. If logs are burning, we see (for, fire, fur).

5. If snow is clean, it is (white, with, wheel).

6. If you are careful, you will be (soft, sail, safe).

D Put a word from the puzzle into each sentence.

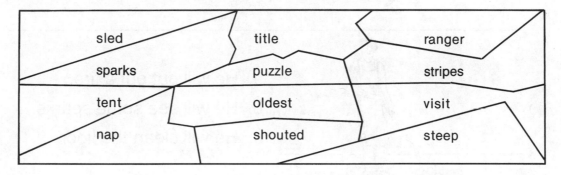

sled	title	ranger
sparks	puzzle	stripes
tent	oldest	visit
nap	shouted	steep

1. We can't find three of the _____ parts.

2. Some _____ from the fire burned the flowers.

3. The baby takes a _____ every morning.

4. What is the _____ of the book you like best?

5. The tiger has black _____.

6. Grandmother is the _____ one in our family.

7. Let's take a _____ to sleep in when we go camping.

8. I want to be a _____ and work in the woods.

9. My aunt is coming to _____ us for a week.

10. The teacher said we _____ when we should have whispered.

What do you think will happen next? <u>Underline</u> the best answer.

1.
   a. He will fix the tire.
   b. He will buy a new bike.
   c. He will paint the tires.

2.
   a. She will get a broom to fix it.
   b. She will get a needle and thread to fix it.
   c. She will ask a mother hen to fix it.

3.
   a. He will put out a fire.
   b. He will see some sparks.
   c. He will clean the floor.

4.
   a. Flowers will grow in them.
   b. They will walk away.
   c. They will get dry.

5.
   a. The pen will get too heavy.
   b. The balloon will get too heavy.
   c. The air will come out of the balloon.

6.
   a. The ball will fly away.
   b. The ball will go up in the air and come back down.
   c. The ball will change into a balloon.

F **Write yes or no after each sentence.**

1. If there is a heavy rain, the ground will get wet. _____

2. If people are flying, they must be on an airplane. _____

3. If grass is growing, it is getting taller. _____

4. If you jump into a swimming pool, you will get dry. _____

5. A ranger is too heavy for you to carry. _____

6. If you want your little brother to go away, put a stamp on him

   and drop him in a mailbox. _____

7. If you are careful, you can build a safe fire. _____

8. Mittens keep people's feet warm. _____

G **What can you learn from these stories? Underline the answer.**

Four children wanted to play a game. But the game box said that six people were needed to play the game.

1. What do we know about playing this game?
   a. The children must get more people to play.
   b. The children do not need more people to play.
   c. They have too many children to play the game.

2. How many children do they still need to get?
   a. four   b. three   c. two   d. no children

Dad was cooking eggs for breakfast. He cooked one egg for each member of the family. There were five in the family. Dad has twelve eggs in the house.

3. What do we know about the eggs?
   a. Dad had eggs left after breakfast.
   b. Dad needed more eggs for breakfast.
   c. There were no eggs for breakfast.

4. How many eggs were left after breakfast?
   a. eight   b. seven   c. three   d. no eggs

H Put these marks " " in the right places to show what was said. Then tell who is talking. If no one is talking, write **no one**. One is done for you.

Ralph   **Donna**   **Liz**   **Detective Sharp Eye**

1. "Hello, Detective Sharp Eye!" said Ralph. _____**Ralph**_____

2. Good afternoon, Ralph, said Detective Sharp Eye.

   _____

3. The children played a game with the detective.

   _____

4. Liz whispered, You are a good detective, Donna.

   _____

5. The detective said, Good detectives must think.

   _____

6. What is wrong in this story, Liz? asked Donna.

   _____

7. She said, Jack looked out of his window at midnight. In the bright sunlight, he saw the robbers behind the barn.

   _____

8. Liz and Ralph thought for a long time. _____

9. Ralph did not answer. _____

10. Jack could not see the robbers in the sunlight. The sun is not

    out at midnight, said Liz. _____

11. Good thinking, Liz, said Donna. _____

Where is Detective Sharp Eye? Use the letters next to the pictures. Put the right letter by each story.

a.

b.

c.

d.

e.

_____ 1. Detective Sharp Eye is very tired. He just pulled off the road to get something fixed on his car. He is resting and waiting for the car to be ready. Then he will drive on.

_____ 2. Detective Sharp Eye is in another place. He must hurry to another city to work. He has a ticket and he is waiting. Soon something will pull up. It will make a lot of noise as it rides on the tracks. It will quickly carry Detective Sharp Eye far away.

_____ 3. Now Mr. Sharp Eye is in a different place. He is getting in line with other people to buy a ticket. They are all going to another town. They will be riding together and resting as the driver takes them along the road. The driver will check the tires before they leave.

_____ 4. Now Detective Sharp Eye is in a small town. He is in a big place with trucks all around him. Each truck is red and some have ladders. Many people work in this place. They put out fires.

Early in the summer, Mark got a new skateboard for his birthday. Since then, he had been on the skateboard every day. He did nothing but practice every hour that he was awake.

Mark's parents made sure that he learned to skateboard on their driveway, where it was safe. They told him that he must always wear long pants and shoes. They also gave him the right safety equipment. He had a helmet, knee pads, elbow pads, and gloves.

Mark was good at sports. In no time, he was better at skateboarding than his friends. "I can't wait around for you snails to learn! I'm too good!" boasted Mark. "I'm going to the skateboard bowl where there are high ramps."

Soon Mark no longer saw his old friends. He was too busy at the ramp talking to the older boys and learning new tricks. The big boys taught him "kick turns," "wheelies," and "lip tricks."

Mark got better and better at skateboarding. Everyone said that he would be a champion some day.

But Mark was not a champ at home. He never helped with any of the work around the house or yard. He never answered when his parents talked to him. He acted as if his little sister Julie was not even there. He did not look at her, help her, or say a word to her.

His school friends did not want to be around Mark. He always boasted about how great he was on the skateboard. He made fun of them all the time because they were not as good as he was.

Mark was so busy thinking of himself that he forgot his family was going to the beach for a week. When Dad reminded him to pack his swimsuit and fins, Mark was upset. "I am not going to that stupid beach!" he shouted. "I do not want to do anything but skateboard!"

Mom shut her ears. She packed Mark's things, but she did not put in any of his skateboard equipment. "We are going to the beach, and so are you," she told Mark.

Once he got to the beach, Mark started to have fun swimming, fishing, and learning to dive. He did not think much about skateboarding until the family went to a mall to shop. Mark saw that a smooth sidewalk went down a hill from the mall to the parking lot. "That hill is perfect for skateboarding," he thought.

Then one day, Eric, a friend Mark had made at the beach, showed Mark his skateboard. Mark grabbed the board from Eric and headed toward the mall.

Eric tried to get his board back. "You can't skateboard," he said to Mark. "You don't have any equipment. You are not even wearing shoes."

But Mark kept going. When they got to the mall, he jumped on the board. He did not even look down the hill to see if there was anything or anyone in the way. ZOOM! ZOOM! Down he went! People jumped out of the way as Mark raced past.

There were some tiny stones on the sidewalk. Mark did not see them. BANG! The skateboard wheels hit the stones! Mark did a backward flip and smashed down on the sidewalk.

It was an awful day for Mark. When he came to, he was at the hospital. He had two broken bones in his left arm, three broken bones in his right arm, and mashed toes on both his feet. The doctor told Mark that toes that get mashed from skateboarding without shoes are called "hamburger toes."

The doctor also said that many skateboarders break their elbow bones. These breaks are called "skateboard elbows." "You're the champion!" the doctor said to Mark. "You've got not one, but <u>two</u> skateboard elbows."

 Underline the right answer to each question.

1. What do we know about Mark?

   a. He helped his sister all the time.

   b. He boasted a lot.

   c. He liked to work in the garden.

   d. He did good work in school.

2. What is this story mainly about?

    a. all the sports Mark liked

    b. a well-liked boy

    c. the water sports at the beach

    d. a person who wanted to do only one thing

3. In no time, Mark learned to skateboard. What does <u>in no time</u> mean?

    a. very slowly

    b. very quickly

    c. never learned

    d. did not have time for

4. What did Mark think of going to the beach with his family?

    a. He did not want to go.

    b. He was ready to go.

    c. He did not want his sister to go.

    d. He did not want his mother to teach him to swim.

5. When his mother "shut her ears," what did she do?

    a. She put on her earmuffs.

    b. She put on her earrings.

    c. She did not let Mark talk.

    d. She did not listen to what Mark said.

6. Why did Mark's parents make him practice in the driveway?

    a. It was safer.

    b. He did not like to leave home.

    c. He had to watch Julie.

    d. He was too little to go to the park.

7. When did Mark start going to the skateboard bowl with the ramps?

    a. before his birthday

    b. after he took Julie to the park

    c. after he could skate well

    d. when his friends became good skaters

8. What equipment did Mark use to protect himself?

   a. helmet, shirt, and shorts

   b. knee pads, socks, and shorts

   c. elbow pads, long pants, vest

   d. helmet, knee pads, elbow pads, and gloves

9. Mark did not want to go to the beach. Why?

   a. He did not like to sit in the sun.

   b. He could not swim.

   c. He wanted to be in school.

   d. He wanted to skateboard all the time.

10. Why did Mark make fun of his old friends?

    a. They learned to skateboard faster than Mark did.

    b. They did not have on their safe equipment.

    c. They did not learn to skateboard as fast as Mark did.

    d. They did not learn to dive as fast as Mark did.

11. What was awful about the last day at the beach?

    a. It rained all day long.

    b. Mark had to sell his skateboard equipment.

    c. Mark hurt himself.

    d. Mark sat in the sun too long and got sick.

12. What helped Mark become so good at skateboarding?

    a. He practiced a lot.   b. His father helped him.

    c. He never practiced.   d. Julie helped him.

13. Why did the doctor say Mark was a champion?

    a. He was a champion skateboarder.

    b. He was the champion of broken bones.

    c. He was the best at breaking skateboards.

    d. He was the best brother Julie could have.

B **To be a champion, you must practice. Here are some of the new words in our story. Read the sentences, learn to read the words, and know their meanings. Then you will be a champ. Circle the right word to finish each sentence.**

1. For every sport, people must have the right
   (everything, equipment, ending).

2. A helmet is used to protect a person's
   (heat, head, heard).

3. To be the best in anything is to be a
   (champion, change, chicken).

4. When you work very hard at learning something, you are
   (protecting, packing, practicing).

5. Every day has twenty-four (ours, hears, hours).

6. When children practice over and over, they get
   (butter, better, basket).

7. When something is very bad, we say it is
   (awful, elbow, always).

8. We do not like people who (bone, boat, boast) too much.

9. A place without steps where you can go up and down is a
   (rack, ramp, read).

10. Mark had several broken (bones, boards, bowls).

11. A part of an arm is an (along, evening, elbow), and a
    part of a leg is a (kick, knee, free).

12. To be hard at work is to be (busy, bus, buzz).

13. Poor Mark! His skateboard hit some (stores, stars, stones),
    and he got (heard, her, hurt).

14. Mark was the champion of the skateboard
    (ends, elbows, every).

C Here is the Table of Contents of a book that Mark and his friends read to learn about skateboarding.

Zip, Zip, Up and Away

Table of Contents

Each chapter of the book tells you something you should know about skateboarding. Under each picture below, write the chapter title and page number that goes with the picture.

1. _____

_____

2. _____

_____

3. _____

_____

4. _____

_____

D Look at the Table of Contents on page 50. In which chapter would each paragraph below be found? After each paragraph, write the chapter title and the page number where the chapter begins.

1. Here are the main styles of this sport. The <u>Streetstyle</u> skateboarder jumps over boxes, bars, or other things while doing tricks. The <u>Freestyle</u> skater skates on flat places while doing tricks. In <u>Ramp skating</u>, the skateboarder skates up on the ramp and does tricks on the top edge, or lip, of the ramp.

Title _____ Page _____

_____ _____

2. One thing to remember is never to ride in and out of traffic on very busy streets. Skateboards are good for moving fast, but only in places where you will not be hit by vans, trucks, or cars. Remember that water and wheels do not mix. It is bad to ride into puddles. The quickest falls happen with wet wheels.

Title _____ Page _____

_____ _____

3. Make sure that your skateboard is always kept in good order. Never ride until you have checked that the wheels are clean and ready to roll. If it happens to start raining as you ride, stop and get off. Put your skateboard into a plastic bag so it will not get wet.

Title _____ Page _____

_____ _____

4. When you first start on your skateboard, find places that are good practice spots. Flat places, your own driveway, and dead-end streets near your home can let you have as much time as you need to become a good skateboarder. Some towns may close streets to traffic for a short time so the skaters have enough room to practice.

Title _____ Page _____

_____ _____

E Choose the correct answer for each question.

Table of Contents or **Dictionary**

1. Which one is in alphabetical order?

_____

2. Which one has meanings of words?

_____

3. Which one has chapters?

_____

4. Which one tells how to say a word?

_____

5. Which one tells the page on which a story begins?

_____

F If you were one of Mark's old friends, and he had boasted and called you a snail, would you forgive him after he was hurt so badly? Would you go over to help him? Write three sentences telling how you would feel. Tell <u>why</u> you would feel that way.

_____

_____

_____

_____

_____

G Poor Mark. He hurts all over. He feels awful too, because he keeps thinking about all the fun he is missing.

It is still summer, and his friends are doing all kinds of fun things. But they have not forgotten Mark. Every day someone comes to help take care of him.

Here are some of the things Mark's friends do. Read the sentences. Look at the pictures. Write the right person's name under each picture.

Erica comes to brush Mark's hair.
Julie feeds him his lunch.
Jack reads sports stories to Mark.
Jenny brushes Mark's teeth for him.
Pam gives him water with a straw.
Ed answers the telephone and takes messages.
When Mark's back starts to itch, Alec scratches it for him.
Mom changes his pajamas for him.

1. _____ 2. _____ 3. _____

4. _____ 5. _____ 6. _____

7. _____ 8. _____ 9. _____

As the class lined up to go to the gym, Emily's heart started to beat faster. She kept saying to herself, "I hate gym. I hate gym."

Emily just was not very good at sports. She tried, but somehow she always did something that made some of the class giggle and some feel sorry for her.

When they played softball, Emily always struck out. She had trouble catching, too. The ball seemed to slip right through her fingers.

Even when she did catch the ball, Emily had trouble throwing it to a player on a base. It usually ended up somewhere out in the field.

Emily thought about this as gym class started. At first, all went well. Mrs. Perkins, the gym teacher, had the children bouncing balls and running in place. No one could see who was doing well and who was not.

Then Mrs. Perkins divided the class into teams. Each member of a team had to take a turn climbing a rope. Emily got in line and waited for her turn.

Tony was in line behind her. "Let's see what you're going to mess up today, Emily," he said quietly. Tony did not want Mrs. Perkins to hear him. She took gym seriously. No laughing! No fooling around! No teasing!

Emily froze. She knew in her heart that Tony was right. She was clumsy. She was going to do something awful. It happened every time.

Emily's best friend, Letty, whispered, "Don't listen to mean old Tony. All you have to do is try to go up the rope a little way. Then just put one hand under the other and come down slowly."

Emily nodded. It was her turn. Mrs. Perkins said, "You can do it, Emily. Don't try too hard. Relax. Climb as high as you feel you can."

Emily went to the rope. She knew she was not good at climbing, but she would try. She thought she could get almost to the top. She started climbing. Up she climbed, like a monkey. She was halfway to the top.

The watching class cheered, "Go, Em, go! Good! Good!"

Emily was pleased by their praise. She relaxed. She slid to the floor.

Several days later, a new boy named Justin entered Emily's class. Justin was tall. He had big muscles and looked as if he would be good at sports. Everyone liked him because he was kind and fun.

"Just wait until Justin sees me in gym, Letty," Emily said. "He'll be making fun of me, too."

On the first gym day for Justin, the class did rolls and handstands on the mats. Cold with fear, Emily did everything without a slip. The class cheered.

When it was Justin's turn, Mrs. Perkins smiled as he came to the mat. Then, as she watched Justin, Mrs. Perkins began to look puzzled.

It seemed Justin could not do a forward roll. He froze. He could do a backward roll, but when he tried a handstand, he flopped over.

Next the class had relay races. Emily raced all the way quickly, picked up the beanbag, and started back to her team. She was almost there when she tripped and fell. She slid to her team, holding the beanbag in front of her.

"At least she got here!" shouted Letty, grabbing the beanbag and running.

The races ended suddenly when Justin tripped on his own shoe and slid into his team. He knocked them all down.

Justin and Emily both felt bad. Now no one would want either one of them on their team.

"That leaves us two together," said Justin. "The last ones chosen."

Emily smiled. It was good to have company. It was better to have a friend.

Underline the right answer to each question.

1. What was Emily's trouble?

   a. She did not think.

   b. She was sick all the time.

   c. She had no friends.

   d. She was clumsy.

2. What is the best meaning for the word <u>usually</u>?

   a. most of the time

   b. seldom

   c. once in a while

   d. never

3. What is the word for a kind of <u>laugh</u>?

   a. smile   b. frown

   c. praise   d. giggle

4. Why did everyone think Justin would be good in sports?

   a. He was fun to play with.

   b. He was kind.

   c. He had big muscles.

   d. He never made mistakes.

5. What happened when Emily climbed the rope?

   a. She could not climb up on the rope.

   b. She got stuck at the top.

   c. Letty had to bring Emily down.

   d. She went up well but came down too fast.

6. What could Justin do?

   a. climb a rope

   b. a backward roll

   c. a handstand

   d. a forward roll

B **Be a good sport. Hit a home run by writing each word next to its correct meaning.**

praise   bounce   relay
usually   relax   clumsy
serious   giggle   muscles

1. a kind of race _____

2. not funny _____

3. to tell how well you do

_____

8. what a ball does

_____

4. to rest

_____

7. always dropping things

_____

5. most of the time _____

6. they help your body move _____

C Every sentence must have two parts: a **who** or **what** part and an **action** part. Read these sentences and <u>underline</u> the **who** or **what** part. Circle the **action** part.

1. Justin can practice.

2. Emily shouted.

3. Up, up went the baseball.

You may add other words or phrases to a sentence to tell <u>**when, where, why,**</u> or <u>**how**</u> something happened.

D A **when** phrase tells the time that the action happens. Look at each picture to find out when the action happened. Finish each sentence with a **when** phrase.

1. Mrs. Bell was driving

_____.

2. Letty was home

_____.

3. The boys and girls played

ball _____.

E A **where** phrase tells the place where the action happened. Write the **where** phrases in these sentences.

1. Julie did a headstand on the mat. Where did Julie do the headstand?

_____

2. The gym was on the first floor. Where was the gym?

_____

Read to find out what Emily and Justin did to become less clumsy. Write the phrases from the story that answer the questions.

The Rest of the Story

1. Every Thursday and Friday, Emily and Justin took swimming lessons at Woodwell Middle School.

   Who or What? _____

   Action? _____

   Where? _____

   When? _____

2. Emily learned to dive into the pool during her second lesson.

   Who or What? _____

   Action? _____

   Where? _____

   When? _____

3. Every morning, Justin does sit-ups in his bedroom.

   Who or What? _____

   Action? _____

   Where? _____

   When? _____

4. Justin's parents took many pictures on the playground the last day of school.

   Who or What? _____

   Action? _____

   Where? _____

   When? _____

G A **why** phrase tells the reason that the action happened. The pictures below show why these things happened. Complete each sentence by writing the correct **why** phrase.

1. I turned on the lights

    _____.

    a. to see better   b. to hear better

2. He got the skates

    _____.

    a. to eat dinner   b. to have fun

3. She put on her helmet

    _____.

    a. to protect her elbows

    b. to protect her head

H A **how** phrase tells in what way an action was done. The pictures below show how some actions happened. Complete each sentence by writing the correct **how** phrase.

1. We walked by the dog

    _____.

    a. very quietly

    b. very noisily

2. She is eating

    _____.

    a. with a fork

    b. with her tongue

3. He moved a large stone

    _____.

    a. with his hands   b. with his car

I Write the answers to the questions below. Then put the parts together to make a good sentence. Write the whole sentence on the lines. Start with a **capital letter** and end with a **period**.

for food   all over the world   kill insects

in the spring   many birds

1. When? _____

   Who or What? _____

   Where? _____

   Action? _____

   Why? _____

   _____

   _____

   _____

across town   every morning   many children

travel   to reach the school   by car and bus

2. When? _____

   Who? _____

   Action? _____

   Where? _____

   How? _____

   Why? _____

   _____

   _____

   _____

J **Here is the end of the story. Read the story and write the correct phrase after each question.**

Emily swims and dives twice a week. In the water, she never trips and falls. She swims to help her become less clumsy. Justin still does sit-ups in the morning and in the evening. He practices to make his muscles strong.

1. <u>Why</u> does Emily swim so much?

    a. to become clumsy

    b. to become less clumsy

    _____

2. <u>Where</u> is Emily less clumsy?

    a. in the water

    b. in the gym

    _____

3. <u>When</u> does Emily swim and dive?

    a. once a week

    b. twice a week

    _____

4. <u>How</u> does Justin keep his muscles strong?

    a. by practicing running

    b. by doing sit-ups

    _____

5. <u>Why</u> does Justin do that?

    a. to run fast and not trip

    b. to get better in sports

    _____

6. <u>When</u> does Justin practice?

    a. twice a day

    b. three times a week

    _____

Lita was sad. The other lizards always crept away when Lita appeared on the tree bark.

"Don't come near us," the lizards said. "You bring our enemies around. They want to eat us."

Lita knew they were right. All the lizards were green, yellow, brown, or tan. All but Lita, she was strange.

Most lizards changed colors to match the trees and leaves where they lived. All but Lita. She could change colors like her friends, but her colors were bright and beautiful.

Most of the time Lita was a beautiful pink. People, birds, and raccoons came crowding around to look at this pretty, strange lizard.

This upset Lita, so her pink changed to scarlet. If she became very, very, VERY upset, she turned bright purple. If there was a cool breeze, her purple color got light blue spots on it.

Many people said, "Oooh, ahhh. What beautiful colors."

Sometimes when animals came to see Lita, they would spot other lizards trying to hide in the leaves. Then they ate a good meal of lizards.

"You brought our enemies here," shouted the other lizards. "But we're the ones that will get gobbled up."

It was true. No animal would taste Lita. Her bright colors might make them sick.

64

All alone Lita felt unloved and unwanted. Even her mother would not come near her.

She was getting very skinny, too. It seemed that even insects went the other way when they spotted the bright lizard. Her long, thin, quick tongue could not catch any insects for food.

"I will ask some other animals how they protect themselves," said Lita. "Then I might be able to help my lizard friends. They might like me again."

First she went to the owl and asked him. He showed her his sharp claws and big beak. No help there!

Then she talked to the goat. He showed her his hard hooves that let him run very fast.

"I have this, too!" he yelled and tried to butt Lita with his sharp horns.

"Some lizards have horns, too," said Lita, "but ours cannot hurt other animals."

The next day Lita asked Mrs. Skunk, "How do you keep your enemies away, Mrs. Skunk?"

Mrs. Skunk laughed, "I'll show you," she said.

Lita was sorry she had asked. Why?

A   <u>Underline</u> **the right answer to each question.**

1. What is this story mainly about?

    a. the work of some lizards

    b. how owls protect themselves

    c. a strange lizard

    d. how skunks protect themselves

2. How did Lita feel when she was left alone?

    a. happy

    b. unloved and unwanted

    c. beautiful

    d. crowded

3. How did Lita's lizard friends try to protect themselves?

    a. by butting their enemies with their horns

    b. by using their sharp claws

    c. by using a bad smell

    d. by matching the colors of trees and leaves

4. What kinds of foods do lizards eat?

    a. insects

    b. seeds

    c. bark of trees

    d. The story does not say.

5. Why was Lita getting skinny?

    a. She was on a diet.

    b. She was not hungry.

    c. All the insects went the other way.

    d. The goat told her not to eat.

6. How do lizards use their tongues?

    a. to clean themselves

    b. to capture food

    c. to tell their families of danger

    d. to smell an enemy

7. What is a lizard's tongue like?

   a. thick and strong and pink

   b. covered with fuzz

   c. long, thick, and flat

   d. long, thin, and fast

8. Lita turned scarlet. What color is that?

   a. bright blue   b. light pink

   c. bright red   d. bright purple

9. When did this story happen?

   a. last year

   b. last week

   c. on a winter evening

   d. The story does not tell.

10. Why didn't other lizards want Lita to come near them?

    a. They said she was too beautiful.

    b. Their enemies came to look at her.

    c. She was mean to them.

    d. She gobbled up her friends.

11. What is the best title for this story?

    a. Loved by All

    b. Nobody's Friend

    c. The Animal With Hooves

    d. Lita's Horns

12. What happened last?

    a. Lizards crept away from Lita.

    b. People said, "Oooh, ahh!"

    c. Lita's beautiful colors brought many enemies near.

    d. Lita talked to a skunk.

B **Find the right word for each meaning. Write the words.**

a. capture   e. crept   i. brought
b. strange   f. gobbled   j. protect
c. hooves   g. taste   k. enemies
d. beautiful   h. beak

1. took something to a friend _____

2. to catch and hold _____

3. to see if something is good to eat _____

4. hard part on goat's feet _____

5. to take care of _____

6. ate fast _____

7. odd, different _____

8. a part of a bird _____

9. very pretty _____

10. those who want to harm _____

 Let's learn about paragraphs.

1. Where does a paragraph start? The first word of a paragraph is
   moved to the right. We say it is indented. Look back at the
   story on pages 64 and 65. How many paragraphs does the story
   have? Write the number. _____

2. Write the first word in paragraph five. _____

3. Write the number of the paragraph that tells what colors the
   other lizards were. _____

4. Write the number of the paragraph that tells what happened
   when Lita got chilly. _____

D **Some words have a part added to them that changes their meaning. If these parts are added at the beginning of the words, they are called prefixes.**

In this story we used the prefix **un**. **Un** means **not**. See how the prefix changes the meaning of these words you know.

tied   untied

The words in the box have prefixes. Write each one in a sentence.

a. unloved	d. unafraid	g. unanswered
b. unread	e. unseen	h. uneaten
c. unkind	f. unlocked	i. unchanged

1. The door was open. It was _____.

2. No one wanted the old doll. She was

   now _____

3. The telephone rang and rang. It went _____.

4. The needles on the pine tree stayed green. They

   were _____.

5. The other lizards were mean to Lita. They

   were _____.

6. No one else would go near the lion, but Patty

   was _____.

7. Bob and Joe ate half the pie. The rest of the pie

   was _____.

8. The ducks did not know the hunters were there. The

   hunters were _____ in the bushes.

9. The books were locked in the trunk. They

   were _____.

E **The main idea of a paragraph tells what the paragraph is about. Most of the information in the paragraph will be about one important idea.**

Read the paragraphs. Answer the questions by checking the correct answer.

1. Some lizards have tongues that not only taste food but smell it. When lizards see food, their long, slender tongues pop out. The tongue is very sticky. Once a bug is caught, it cannot get away.
This paragraph is mainly about

_____ a. kinds of foods lizards eat

_____ b. the mouths of lizards

_____ c. how lizards use their tongues

2. A lizard has three parts. First, there is a head. Then there is a long body. Last of all it has a long tail. The body is held up on four short legs. Each foot has five toes on it. The toes help the animal stick to branches and tree trunks.
This paragraph mainly tells

_____ a. how lizards travel

_____ b. something about a lizard's looks

_____ c. where lizards live

3. There are many insects found in the warm places where most lizards live. Lizards make bugs their main food. Sometimes it is hard to capture quick, little insects. Then a hungry lizard may even chew on leaves or flowers.
This paragraph mainly tells about a lizard's

_____ a. shape   _____ b. home   _____ c. food

F Most paragraphs have a topic sentence which tells the information to be found in the paragraph. The other sentences in the paragraph give details that tell more about the topic. Read the paragraphs. Find the topic sentences. Sometimes a topic sentence may be the first sentence. Sometimes a topic sentence may be the last sentence.

Underline the topic sentence in each paragraph.

1. Owls are the greatest mouse and rat hunters in the world. When owls look for food in the dark, their big eyes can spot rats and mice moving about. The owl swoops down to catch the smaller animal in its claws. Then it swallows it whole. Farmers love owls because they kill so many rats and mice.

2. Goats do not like to be fenced in. They try to get out of any place they are put in. They want to be free to snoop. They climb rocks and taste every bush they find. They see what they can discover in piles of trash and garbage. They snack on everything. Goats are interesting, funny animals.

G Read the stories in **F** again. Copy each topic sentence. Under the topic sentence, write two details which give more information about the topic.

Topic sentence 1 _____

_____

1. _____

2. _____

Topic sentence 2 _____

_____

1. _____

2. _____

About a week later, Lita was still trying to find a good way to protect herself. She couldn't change her colors to match the trees and leaves like the other lizards.

Lita saw a strange forest animal. It was covered with sharp quills.

"I'm a porcupine," he bragged. "We are mighty animals in these woods. We are left alone. No one dreams of eating us. No one dares to hit us."

"You are lucky," said Lita.

"Just give me a little touch with your long tail," said the porcupine.

Lita shook her head. She turned scarlet because she was so afraid.

"Make me angry!" begged the porcupine. "I can't stick you if I'm not mad."

Just then Lita unrolled her long, thin tongue to capture a passing fly. Seeing Lita stick out her tongue made the porcupine turn his back in anger. He backed up to a small bush. He bumped into the bush.

Lita turned purple! A porcupine quill stuck in every place his back touched.

"You <u>are</u> strong, mighty, and safe from enemies!" said Lita.

Lita heard noises nearby. Beavers were chopping down a large tree. Lita stared! The beavers were chopping with big, strong teeth.

"Do not listen to that bragging porcupine," said Mrs. Beaver. "If you want safety, come to visit us."

Mrs. Beaver showed Lita how her family worked together. They found a stream. The beavers bit down trees and cut the wood into small pieces. Out of the wood they made a strong wall called a dam. The dam cut off part of the stream. That part of the water became a still pond where beaver families could live safely.

"We build strong houses in this pond," bragged Mrs. Beaver. "We can live under the water. No one touches us in this safe pond."

All at once, Mrs. Beaver began to bang her flat tail on the ground. She had seen danger! Some people were near. All the other beavers stopped working. Into the water they plopped. In ten seconds, every beaver was under the water, safe from enemies.

Lita knew she could not bang her tail like a beaver. She did not have quills like the porcupine. She could not let out a bad smell like a skunk. She did not have sharp claws like an owl nor horns like a goat.

Then Lita looked into the pond for her beaver friends. What did she see? She saw a beautiful, bright pink animal looking up at her.

"Is that me?" asked Lita. "Why, I am beautiful!" Lita now knew that her beauty was her protection from enemies. She did not have to be like a beaver, porcupine, skunk, owl, goat, or other lizards. She could just be herself! She did not feel sad anymore.

Underline the right answer to each question.

1. What protects a porcupine?

   a. a sharp tongue

   b. sharp quills

   c. hooves on feet

   d. a flat tail

2. Why did Mrs. Beaver slap her tail on the ground?

   a. She was protecting her enemies.

   b. The tree was falling down.

   c. It was dinner time.

   d. She knew danger was near.

3. Why did the porcupine get mad at Lita?

   a. He thought Lita stuck her tongue out at him.

   b. Lita touched him with her tail.

   c. Lita turned purple.

   d. Lita was a friend of the beaver.

4. When do porcupines use their quills?

   a. never

   b. when they are angry

   c. when they are hungry

   d. when they are happy

5. How do porcupines move to protect themselves?

   a. from side-to-side

   b. rolled into a ball

   c. forward

   d. backward

6. Why do beavers make dams?

    a. to capture many fish

    b. to clean their teeth

    c. to have food for the winter

    d. to have a safe place for their homes

7. What is the main idea of this story?

    a. A lizard has no way of protecting itself.

    b. Each kind of animal has a different way to protect itself.

    c. All animals protect themselves in the same way.

    d. All animals living in ponds are safe from enemies.

8. Why didn't Lita know she was beautiful?

    a. No one told her.

    b. The beaver said she was ugly.

    c. She had never seen herself before.

    d. The porcupine said she was ugly.

9. What happened last?

    a. The beavers plopped into the pond.

    b. The porcupine hit the bush.

    c. Lita saw herself in the pond.

    d. Lita did not want to touch the porcupine.

10. What was Lita's protection from enemies?

    a. her tongue   b. her horns

    c. the beaver's home   d. her bright colors

11. What would happen if Lita dared to touch the porcupine?

    a. Quills would stick her.

    b. The porcupine would be scared.

    c. She would change into a porcupine.

    d. Nothing would happen to her.

B **Finish each sentence with a word from the word box.**

--- Word Box ---
scarlet	bragged	dare
anger	shook	touch
begged	quills	dam

1. The beavers' _____ was a wall to hold back water.

2. If we want to be safe, we would not _____ to cross a street without looking for cars.

3. Lita _____ her friends to stay with her.

4. The _____ were sharp stickers.

5. The strong man _____ that he could lift a car by himself.

6. The flags were white and _____.

7. The porcupine turned his back in _____.

8. If you _____ a beaver's fur, it feels soft and thick.

C **The prefix un means not. Write the prefix un before each of these words to change their meanings.**

a. _____ opened   c. _____ changed   e. _____ afraid

b. _____ covered   d. _____ locked

Match each word to its meaning. Write the letter of each new word in the blank next to its meaning.

1. not scared   _____

2. stayed just the same   _____

3. never been opened   _____

4. opened up with a key   _____

5. took the quilt off   _____

D **Read the story. Then answer the question at the bottom of the page.**

Cutting Down Trees

Before building homes, beavers always make a dam. First, they must cut down trees. Each beaver chews at a different tree. They chew all around it.

When the branches of a tree begin to shake, the beaver working on that tree slaps its tail on the ground. That tells the others to get out of the way so as not to be crushed by the falling tree.

Two or three more bites, and the tree is down.

Now the group must chop the large tree into smaller pieces. They use their strong teeth for this job, too.

How does a beaver chop down a tree? Put the steps in the right order. One is done for you.

a. The tree shakes a little.
b. Other beavers get out of the way.
c. The tree falls.
d. The beaver takes the last bite.
e. The beaver chews all around the tree trunk.
f. The beaver warns the others.

1. **The beaver chews all around the tree trunk.**

2. _____

3. _____

4. _____

5. _____

6. _____

E When did these things happen? Write the word **before** or **after** on the line for each phrase. One is done for you.

1. When did the beavers build a dam?

   ___**before**___ they built a house

2. When did the tree fall?

   _____ beavers got out of the way

3. When do the branches start to shake?

   _____ the tree is ready to fall

4. When does a beaver slap its tail on the ground to warn others?

   _____ the tree comes down

5. When do beavers chew a tree into smaller pieces?

   _____ the tree falls

F Synonyms are words that mean almost the same thing. **Small** and **little** are synonyms. Can you find the synonyms below? Draw lines to match them. One is done for you.

1. big		a. close
2. mighty		b. quick
3. near		c. large
4. rocks		d. stones
5. woods		e. angry
6. fast		f. forest
7. mad		g. strong

78

Match the correct animal with the picture of its body part.

1. goat

2. owl

3. lizard

4. skunk

5. porcupine

6. beaver

Amy Octopus never came up to the top of the ocean. She lived very close to the bottom. Her home was in a crack between large rocks. Amy could make her soft round body very long and thin. Then she could slide into the crack in the rocks. When she was inside the crack, only her beautiful green eyes peeped out from the rocks.

Amy had eight long arms called tentacles to wave around. She used the tentacles to walk, to get food, and to swim about in the water.

One day some scientists stopped their ship right over Amy's home. The scientists wanted to find out how smart an octopus could be. They knew that octopuses could be found in this part of the ocean. But they did not know what a surprise they were going to have!

First, the scientists dropped clams into the water. The clams were hidden under thick seaweed. It took nine minutes for Amy to see the clams, ooze out of her crack, open the clam shells with her arms, and eat the clams. All that time a hidden camera was taking Amy's picture. Amy knew the camera was there. She was a smart octopus!

Next, the scientists gave Amy a harder test. They put the clams into a box and dropped the box to the ocean floor. Amy took eleven minutes to flip open the box and have another meal.

"That's the smartest octopus in the world!" said all the scientists.

The scientists gave Amy something even harder to do. They put a crab into a plastic bag and dropped it. Amy took thirteen minutes to rip open the bag with her tentacles and eat the crab. Then the scientists tried some very hard tests.

"An octopus is such a clever animal!" said the scientists. They took many more pictures of Amy.

They put crabs into a jar with a tight lid on top. They dropped the jar into the ocean. In a short time, Amy used her tentacles to turn the lid and get the jar open. That was Amy's hardest job.

The scientists wanted more people to see how clever Amy was. They asked other scientists from all over the world to come and watch Amy. People came by helicopter from near and far.

They did not know Amy was getting fat from all the food. Amy found it hard to fit back into her crack in the rocks. When the scientists dropped another jar full of crabs to the ocean floor, Amy did not move! All the scientists waited, and waited, and waited. But nothing happened! Amy was so full of food that she was on a diet!

Are you as smart as Amy Octopus? Read these questions carefully. <u>Underline</u> the right answer for each question.

1. Where did Amy live?

   a. close to the bottom of the ocean

   b. on the shore near the ocean

   c. at the top of the ocean

   d. on a ship in the middle of the sea

2. What was Amy's home?

   a. a plastic bag on the ocean floor

   b. a tiny space between seaweed plants

   c. a hole in a ship

   d. a small crack in the rocks

3. What are tentacles?

   a. the eyes of an octopus

   b. the legs of a whale

   c. the arms of an octopus

   d. the cameras of scientists

4. Why were scientists taking pictures of Amy?

   a. to learn how to trap an octopus

   b. to learn more about an octopus

   c. to find treasures on the ocean floor

   d. to learn about seaweed

5. What was the first thing Amy did for the scientists?

   a. learned how to use a camera

   b. learned to talk

   c. found clams hidden in the seaweed

   d. learned how to take pictures out of a camera

6. How did Amy <u>ooze</u> out of the crack in the rocks?

   a. She shot out. b. She hit.

   c. She slid out. d. She jumped.

7. What happened last?

   a. The scientists waited and waited.

   b. Amy turned the lid and opened the jar.

   c. The scientists came by helicopter.

   d. Amy opened a box.

8. What do you think will happen later to Amy?

   a. Amy will never eat again.

   b. The scientists will take Amy away from her home.

   c. Amy will get hungry and start eating again.

   d. Amy will rip up the pictures of herself.

9. Why did Amy stop eating?

   a. Her teeth were hurting too much.

   b. She had eaten too much and was getting heavy.

   c. She did not like the food the scientists had given her.

   d. She did not want the camera to take pictures of her.

10. What did Amy do that most animals could never do?

    a. She ate many different kinds of food.

    b. She hid where no one could find her.

    c. She fixed a broken camera.

    d. She turned the lid of the jar.

11. What is the best title for this story?

    a. Ocean Life

    b. A Ship Full of Scientists

    c. A Clever Animal

    d. The Story of a Fish

B **Let's review paragraphs.**

1. Remember that each paragraph is indented.
2. A paragraph has a main idea or topic. Most paragraphs have a **topic sentence** that tells what the paragraph is about. The other sentences in the paragraph tell more about the topic.

Look back at the story on pages 80 and 81 to answer these.

1. Count how many paragraphs are in the story. Write a number starting with **one** to the left of each paragraph. How many paragraphs are there? _____

2. What are the first and last words of the second paragraph?
   _____   _____

3. Write the last sentence of paragraph four.
   _____

4. Write the last sentence of paragraph ten.
   _____
   _____

5. Copy the paragraph that has only one sentence.
   _____
   _____

6. Write the topic sentence of paragraph eleven.
   _____
   _____

7. Write the topic sentence of paragraph nine.
   _____

8. Write the topic sentence of paragraph five.
   _____

C **The topic sentence is missing from each paragraph. Pick the best topic sentence from the Topic Box. Write it.**

Topic Box
a. An octopus is careful when it looks for a home.
b. The octopus looks very interesting to us.
c. Other animals are also found in the ocean.
d. The octopus can be found in almost any ocean.
e. The octopus finds many foods in the ocean.

1 _____

_____

_____. An octopus eats crabs and clams. It likes all kinds of shellfish.

2 _____

_____. It finds a home in tiny places in the rocks. It likes to have its home well hidden. If an octopus sees a dark cave, it will move in.

3 _____

_____

_____. Many different kinds of fish live there. They are all different colors and shapes. Animals that need air, such as seals and whales, live there, too.

4 _____

_____

_____. It has a soft body with no bones or shell. Eight long arms and two big eyes stick out from its body. The octopus can even change color to look blue, brown, gray, purple, red, or white.

D **Now you are ready to be a writer. Use these topic sentences. Write two more sentences to fit the topic. Write good paragraphs that others will want to read.**

Two little children wanted to play with the same toy.

_____

_____

_____

Heavy rain made the ship toss and turn on the water.

_____

_____

_____

E **These paragraphs have one or more sentences that do not fit the topic. Make each paragraph better. Draw a line through any sentence that does not fit the topic.**

Children need heavy clothes to keep warm when days are cold and icy. Their fingers and toes must be well covered. Children should have thick boots for their feet and heavy gloves for their hands. People like to eat hot soup in the winter. Children also need to wear heavy coats when they go outdoors.

_____

A submarine is a kind of boat that moves under the water. It can move up and down or back and forth near the ocean floor. People eat ham, lettuce, and tomato on their submarine sandwiches. When a submarine is under the water, people in it cannot see to the top of the water. They use a to see what is above the ocean. Plants grow on the ocean floor, too. Submarines can even move under ice in very cold oceans.

F **Write each word on the line beside its meaning.**

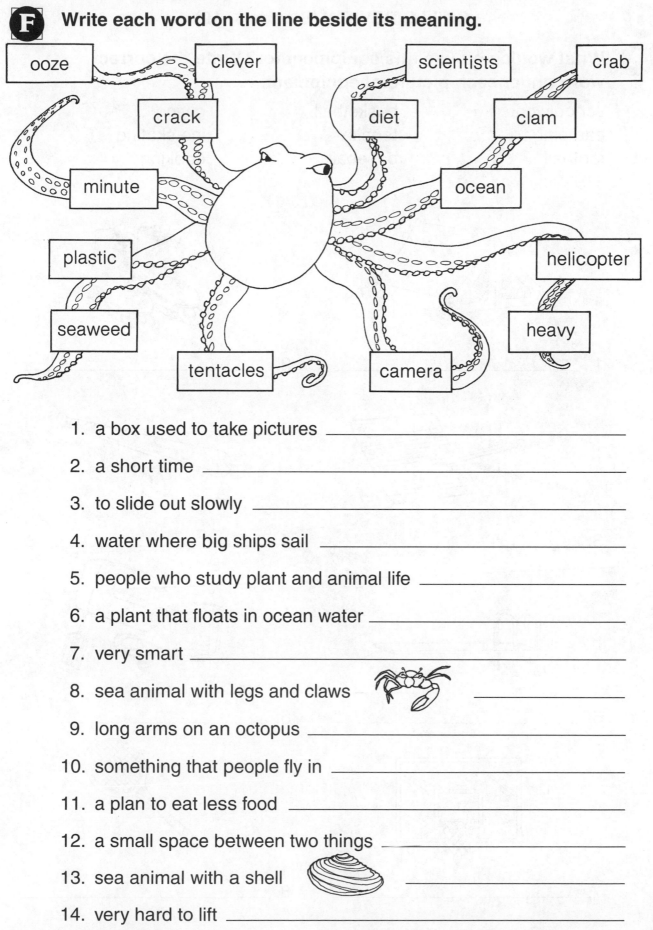

ooze clever scientists crab

crack diet clam

minute ocean

plastic helicopter

seaweed heavy

tentacles camera

1. a box used to take pictures _____

2. a short time _____

3. to slide out slowly _____

4. water where big ships sail _____

5. people who study plant and animal life _____

6. a plant that floats in ocean water _____

7. very smart _____

8. sea animal with legs and claws _____

9. long arms on an octopus _____

10. something that people fly in _____

11. a plan to eat less food _____

12. a small space between two things _____

13. sea animal with a shell _____

14. very hard to lift _____

SKILLS REVIEW (Stories 6–10)

 A What would you use this equipment for? Write the correct word under each picture of equipment.

schoolwork	basketball	diving
camping	tennis	ice skating
football	baseball	cooking

1. _____

2. _____

3. _____

4. _____

5. _____

6. _____

7. _____

8. _____

88

Practice! Practice! Practice! The more you practice, the better you are in reading. Choose the correct word to finish each sentence. Write the word on the blank lines.

1. The knee pads will (practice, protect, praise) your knee bones if you fall.

_____

2. The octopus opened a (porcupine, protect, plastic) bag.

_____

3. Emily was pleased when Mrs. Perkins (practiced, plastic, praised) her.

_____

4. Justin always (ready, relaxed, really) by reading funny stories.

_____

5. Someone who wants to hurt him is his (enemy, equipment, every).

_____

6. Mark (bounced, brought, boasted) his equipment to the skateboard ramp.

_____

7. Children who do good work are (stupid, serious, scientist) about doing their homework.

_____

8. When Ann got to second (base, bake, back), she had to slide in.

_____

C Can you find the phrase that tells who or what the sentence is about? <u>Underline</u> each **who** or **what** phrase.

1. Amy Octopus hid in a crack in the rocks.

2. Bang, bang went the beaver's tail.

3. The scientists gave Amy some hard tests.

4. "Help!" yelled Sam.

5. Lita came down the tree.

6. All porcupines have quills.

D Now let's find the action phrases. Sometimes only one word is needed to tell the action. Circle the part that tells the **action.**

1. Emily and Justin laughed.

2. His arm bone got broken.

3. One girl fell down in the relay race.

4. The rain came faster and faster.

5. People skated and practiced.

6. The lizards changed color.

E Read the story. In what order did things happen? Draw a line from the question to the right answer.

Mr. Bear had not visited the stream for many months. One evening he was hungry. He remembered that he always got lots of fish at one place in the stream. But this time he found the stream was almost dry. There had been no rain for a year. Fish were gone. Mr. Bear had to go to sleep hungry.

1. What came first?   a. Fish could not live in the stream anymore.

2. What came second?   b. No rain fell for a year.

3. What came third?   c. Mr. Bear could not find fish.

4. What came fourth?   d. Water in the stream got lower.

F **Read the names of animals below. Find the name for each picture. Write the animal's name under the picture.**

a. bear   b. bee   c. crab   d. duck
e. frog   f. owl   g. seal   h. tiger

Animals have different kinds of feet because of the different ways they live. Many animals that live in water have webbed feet like these to help them swim better.

1.   2.   3.

_____   _____   _____

Some animals have paws with sharp nails called claws. Claws like these help animals dig, hold onto things, and catch other animals to eat.

4.   5.   6.   7.

_____ _____ _____ _____

G **Draw a line through any sentence that does not go with the topic sentence of this paragraph.**

Bears are always searching for food. Bears eat almost anything they run into. When they come to a stream, they know how to catch as many fish as they want. Bears have white, brown, or black fur. Bears kill and eat any smaller animals they find in the forest. Bears love sweet food. When they find a beehive, they can't wait to eat. They chew up the honey and the bees! Long ago, people used bear skins for rugs.

91

There was a time when ships had no engines. Large ships that crossed the oceans of the world had only sails to make them go. When the wind did not blow to push the sails, the ships could not move along.

On April 3, 1769, a ship named the *Mary Lee* set sail from the West Indies to Boston. The boat was crowded with twenty-three sailors, the captain, and ten passengers.

Two of the passengers were children named John and Margaret Scott. They were traveling with their parents. John and Margaret always wanted to know how long they had been sailing.

Mr. Scott said, "Cut a thick, deep line on this stick every day at sunset. Then you will know how many days we have been on the ocean."

Traveling was hard in 1769. Some passengers were seasick. Sleeping places were crowded, smelly, and had little air. On the twelfth day of the trip, a sailor named Sam fell into the ocean. Sam had been climbing up the mainsail when he fell off.

Some of the sailors rushed to get ropes to throw to Sam. Sam was splashing in the deep water. Most of the people were watching Sam. Mr. Scott was the first to see the giant fin of a huge fish sticking out of the water.

"Danger!" yelled Mr. Scott. "Sharks!"

The shark's fin came through the water faster than the boat could travel.

"Hurry with the ropes!" everyone was yelling.

The shark's fin was close to Sam when three ropes hit the water near him. One rope fell almost into Sam's hands. He grabbed it and held on. The sailors pulled hard on the other end of the rope. Sam was almost up to the ship.

But the huge shark leaped out of the water to bite Sam's leg. People looked into the shark's open mouth and saw two rows of sharp teeth.

Just then Margaret threw the stick at the shark. The shark bit the stick as the sailors pulled Sam up to the deck of the ship. Sam was safe!

Mr. Scott was proud of his children. He let them count the days by making the cuts on the lid of their clothes trunk.

Ⓐ Underline the right answer to each question.

1. When did this story take place?

    a. last year

    b. a long time ago

    c. ten months ago

    d. at sunset every day

2. How many people were on this ship?

    a. twenty-four   b. thirty
    c. twenty-eight   d. thirty-four

3. How did sailboats move through the water?

   a. The sailboats had strong engines.

   b. Sailors pulled them on ropes.

   c. Wind pushed the sails to make boats move.

   d. The sails and the engines pushed the boats.

4. Why did John and Margaret cut lines on a stick?

   a. to count the days

   b. to make toys

   c. to tie ropes together

   d. to know what time it was

5. What was this story about?

   a. how sharks get food

   b. a trip on a sailing ship

   c. how to travel to the West Indies

   d. how to travel on a river

6. How did Sam get back on the ship?

   a. Sailors went to get him in a small boat.

   b. Sailors jumped into the water to get him.

   c. The shark pushed Sam back onto the ship.

   d. Sam held onto a rope and was pulled up.

7. What did the shark want to do with Sam?

   a. use the sailor for food

   b. help Sam back onto the ship

   c. catch the ropes for Sam

   d. make friends with Sam

8. What did not happen to Sam?

   a. He was pulled onto the ship.

   b. He fell into the deep water.

   c. The shark bit him on the leg.

   d. He splashed in the deep water.

9. Where was the ship going?

   a. to the West Indies

   b. to Florida

   c. to Boston

   d. to New York

10. Who was *Mary Lee*?

   a. John Scott's sister

   b. John Scott's mother

   c. a passenger

   d. the ship

11. Which one happened first?

   a. Sam was pulled onto the sailboat.

   b. The shark leaped high out of the water.

   c. The sailors threw ropes to Sam.

   d. People looked into the shark's mouth.

12. What would John and Margaret use today to know the date?

   a. a clock

   b. a stick

   c. a rope

   d. a calendar

13. When did the children cut a deep line on the stick?

   a. every evening

   b. every morning

   c. every week

   d. every hour

14. What is the best title for this story?

   a. How the Shark Helped Sam

   b. Sailing to the West Indies

   c. A Trip on a Steamboat

   d. A Trip on a Sailing Ship

B Can you answer these questions about time?

1. What was the date when the *Mary Lee* set sail? _____

2. How many years ago was that? To work it out:

   a. Write the number of this year's date. _____

   b. Now write the date of the year when the *Mary Lee* set sail. _____

   c. Take the smaller number from the larger number. Now you know how long ago it was. _____ years

3. In 1869 a steamship called the *American Dragon* sailed from Boston to the West Indies.

   a. How many years ago was that trip? _____

   b. How many years after the *Mary Lee* did the *American Dragon* sail? _____

C Choose the right word to write beside the meaning.

a. captain	b. crowded	c. engine	d. shark
e. traveling	f. mainsail	g. parents	h. always
i. passengers	j. trunk	k. seasick	l. fin

1. _____ machine that makes a car or boat move

2. _____ people who ride on boats, cars, or buses

3. _____ the one who gives orders on a ship

4. _____ a box to hold clothes

5. _____ going from place to place

6. _____ largest sail on a ship

7. _____ part of a fish that helps it move

8. _____ filled with people or things

9. _____ a large fish with sharp teeth

10. _____ a mother and father

11. _____ every time

D These lists will help you answer the questions. <u>Underline</u> the right word or fill in the blank to tell when something happened.

Times of Day	Longer Times
1. dawn (sunrise, sunup)	7 days = 1 week
2. morning	4 weeks = 1 month
3. noon	12 months = 1 year
4. afternoon	
5. evening (sunset, sundown)	
6. night	
7. midnight	

1. The passengers could not take baths on the ship. They washed their faces and hands each day just after **sunrise**. When did they wash?

   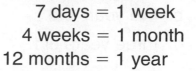

   a. early in the morning

   b. early in the evening

   c. late at night

2. At **dawn**, the sailors woke up and got back to work. When did the sailors wake up?

   a. at sunset

   b. at sunrise

   c. at sundown

3. After **two weeks** on the ship, Mrs. Scott washed some clothes because they had no clean ones left to wear. When did she wash clothes?

   a. after twenty-one days

   b. after seven days

   c. after fourteen days

4. Margaret started making a quilt in **1769**. She finished it in **1771**. How long did it take her to make the quilt?

   a. two months

   b. two years

   c. two weeks

5. Sam, the sailor, got new boots in **1766**. He was still wearing those boots when he fell in the ocean in **1769**. How old were Sam's boots?

   a. a year old

   b. five years old

   c. three years old

6. They had been traveling on the ship for **three weeks**. They asked the captain how much longer the trip would take. He said, "We should get to Boston in **one more week**." How long will the trip take in all?

   a. about one year

   b. about one month

   c. about one week

7. John and Margaret marked off the days at sea by making a cut on a stick each day at **sunset**. When did they mark the stick?

   a. as the sky was getting light

   b. as it was getting dark

   c. at noon when the sun was high in the sky

8. **A year** after they sailed to Boston, Mr. and Mrs. Scott saw some people who had been on the same ship. They talked about the long, hard trip. When did they talk?

   a. twelve weeks after the trip

   b. twelve months after the trip

   c. twelve days after the trip

9. John Scott was born in **1761**. Margaret Scott was born in **1757**.

   a. Which child is older? _____

   b. Which one was eight years old when they sailed on the

      Mary Lee in 1769? _____

   c. How old was Margaret in 1769? _____

E What is a sentence? It can be long or short. But it is only a sentence if it has these two parts. One part tells **who** or **what** the sentence is about. The other part tells the **action** that the "who" or "what" does. These two parts of the sentence are called **phrases**.

1. What does one sentence part tell? _____

2. What does the other part tell? _____

3. What are sentence parts called? _____

F Read these sentences. <u>Underline</u> the phrase that tells **who** or **what** in each sentence. Then ⃝circle the **action** phrase. One is done for you.

1. <u>Fish</u> ⟨can swim.⟩

2. The wind blew harder.

3. The ship is turning.

4. Sam fell down.

5. Margaret ran quickly.

6. A sailor pulled hard.

G These groups of words look like sentences, but some are not. One phrase is missing in some of them. Put a capital **S** by each one that is a sentence.

_____ 1. Pulled hard on the ropes.

_____ 2. Passengers on the ship were seasick.

_____ 3. Sailor Sam fell off the mainsail.

_____ 4. A big school of fish.

_____ 5. Will get to Boston in one week.

_____ 6. The ship moved slowly.

_____ 7. They made a cut on the stick each day.

Read the story. Then answer the questions.

A long time ago, a ship could not leave port until high tide. Low tide means the water is not deep. A ship could get stuck on the sand at the bottom. High tide means the water is much deeper. The ship can float without touching bottom.

On April 3, 1769, the *Mary Lee* was waiting for high tide. The captain and the sailors knew when the tides changed.

The captain watched how deep the water was. He ordered the crew to set sail. Sailors began to climb the ropes. They let out the sails and got them ready. John, Margaret, and the other passengers waved good-bye to their friends.

One sailor stood by the wheel ready to steer the ship. The wind filled the sails and pushed the ship forward. The sailor at the wheel began to steer the ship.

When did these things happen? Write the word **before** or **after** on the line for each phrase.

1. When did the captain order the ship to sail?

    _____ the sailor began to steer

2. When did the crew climb the ropes?

    _____ they let out the sail

3. When did the ship sail?

    _____ the tide was high

4. When did the passengers wave good-bye?

    _____ the ship sailed away

5. When did the *Mary Lee* sail?

    _____ April 10, 1769

6. When did the sails fill out?

    _____ the captain knew the water was deep enough

Read each question. Draw a line to the right answer.

1. What came first?

2. What came second?

3. What came third?

4. What came last?

a. A sailor steered the boat out of the port.

b. Sailors let out the sails.

c. The tide got high.

d. The captain ordered the ship to sail.

Use these topic sentences. Write two more sentences that fit each topic. Make good paragraphs that others will want to read.

Amy found $5.00 on the school playground. _____

_____

_____

_____

Rusty was having a hard time learning to ride the pony. _____

_____

_____

_____

A box fell off the truck when it turned the corner. _____

_____

_____

_____

12

Several days had passed since Sam, the sailor, was saved from the shark. Then another serious thing happened to the sailing ship. The wind just stopped blowing! With no wind, the *Mary Lee* could not move ahead. It just drifted slowly about. The captain told the sailors to change the sails to catch any light breeze. But no air stirred.

John Scott said, "Maybe the wind will spring up again when it gets dark."

"I hope so," said Mrs. Scott. "It is so hot and still without a breeze blowing."

The sun went down in the west. Darkness crept over the water but still no wind blew. People began to hope that by dawn a breeze would spring up to send them on their way.

At dawn the sun appeared again and it began to get light. But still there was no wind. So it went, day after day. No wind blew and the sails just hung.

Then things became more serious. There was not much water left to drink. The food that should have been enough for the whole trip was running low. The passengers and crew were hot, hungry, tired, and afraid. They could see sharks' fins swimming around the ship.

"Blow, wind!" cried Margaret. "It is strange. At home I used to hate strong wind because it blew my bonnet off my head!"

John said, "Before we got on the ship, I hoped that we would never have storm winds. I was afraid winds would push huge waves over the ship and wash us into the ocean."

Night hours were bad times for the passengers and crew. They were running low on candles. The captain would not let them light the candles after dark. When people could not sleep, they had to sit in the dark and wait for dawn to come.

Each day the sailors put fishing lines over the sides of the ship to catch fish. Often sharks swam over and pulled some of the fish off the hooks.

Just when everyone had almost given up hope, one morning tiny drops of rain began to come down. A light breeze stirred and the rain fell harder. Then the wind pushed against the sails. Slowly the boat turned and was on its way again.

The captain said, "If the wind keeps blowing, we'll be in Boston in one week." Everyone was happy to hear that.

At sunset, Margaret made one more heavy cut in the lid of the trunk. She showed it to John.

John said, "It seems as if we have been on this ship for years, but it has only been twenty-one days!"

A **Underline the right answer to each question.**

1. What do you think might happen **now** if the wind stopped blowing around a large passenger ship?

    a. People would run low on food and water.

    b. People would have to radio for help.

    c. Helicopters would pull the ship along.

    d. Nothing would happen.

2. How long did they wait for the wind to blow again?

    a. nine hours   b. eight months

    c. three years   d. many days

3. How did they know that sharks were nearby?

    a. Fins were sticking out of the water.

    b. They heard the noises of the sharks.

    c. Divers saw sharks when they swam under the ship.

    d. Another ship warned them about the sharks.

4. Why did Margaret hate the strong winds on land?

    a. The wind blew her off her feet.

    b. The wind blew her hat off.

    c. The wind made the waves too high.

    d. The wind kept her from traveling.

5. The air stirred. What does this mean?

    a. The air moved.

    b. The wind stood still.

    c. The ship made the wind blow.

    d. They waved a spoon in the air.

6. How did the captain try to get the ship moving?

    a. He told the crew to fix the engines.

    b. He told the crew to change clothes.

    c. He had the sailors row the ship.

    d. He had the sailors change the sails.

7. What was the danger in not sailing on for so long?

    a. The ship could turn over quicker.

    b. The people got tired of waiting to sail on.

    c. The people did not have enough air.

    d. They would not have enough food and water.

8. Why couldn't they get water to drink from the ocean?

    a. Sharks would not let them get near the water.

    b. Ocean water is not good for drinking.

    c. They might get fish in their mouths from ocean water.

    d. The waves were not high enough.

9. How could they get more food while the ship was still?

    a. from other ships passing by

    b. by growing it in some dirt

    c. by catching fish

    d. by helicopter

10. What can we learn from this story?

    a. Sharks have a hard time finding food in the ocean.

    b. Ocean travel took a long time on a sailing ship.

    c. People should not travel on ships.

    d. People saw more when they traveled by ship.

11. What do you think might have happened if there had been no strong wind for several months?

    a. The people would have died because they had no water.

    b. The sharks would have eaten the ship.

    c. The sailing ship would have turned over and sunk.

    d. Other ships would have pulled the *Mary Lee* along.

12. What is the best title for this story?

    a. Saving the Candles

    b. Running Out of Food

    c. How the Wind Blows

    d. A Sailing Ship Without Wind

 Write the answers to these questions about time.

1. How many days had the Scotts been on the ship by the end of the story? _____

2. How many weeks was that? _____

3. They had to travel one more week to reach Boston. How many weeks did the trip take in all? _____

4. When Columbus sailed to the New World, the trip took ten weeks. How many days did that trip take? _____

5. Columbus sailed in 1492. The Scotts sailed in 1769.

    a. Which trip came first? _____

    b. How many years were there between the two trips? _____

C **Which are times of day and which are times of night? Put the right words on the sails of each ship.**

a. morning   b. dawn   c. evening   d. darkness

e. noon   f. bedtime   g. midnight   h. sunrise

1.   2.

Day Times   Night Times

D   **Draw lines to match the words and meanings.**

1. one week   a. name of a month

2. twenty-eight days   b. twenty-one days

3. twelve months   c. fourteen days

4. three weeks   d. four weeks

5. Tuesday   e. one year

6. two weeks   f. one day of the week

7. August   g. a date long ago

8. April 3, 1769   h. seven days

E   (Circle) **the right answer to each question.**

1. John made another cut on the stick each day at **sunset**.
   When did he do this?

   a. noon   b. midnight   c. evening   d. dawn

2. The storm began at **dawn**. When did the storm start?

   a. early morning   b. early evening

   c. late evening   d. late afternoon

3. The wind stopped blowing at **sunrise**. When did it stop?

   a. midnight   b. dawn   c. evening   d. noon

4. Sam climbed the ropes to the top of the sails at **noon**.
   When did he climb the ropes?

   a. as darkness fell   b. early morning

   c. at sunrise   d. middle of the day

5. They ate fish at **sundown**. When did they eat?

   a. dawn   b. early evening

   c. late morning   d. middle of the day

6. The ship traveled faster at **night**. When did it go faster?

   a. early morning   b. before sunset

   c. after sunset   d. at dawn

F How careful a reader are you? Did these things happen long ago or could they happen now? Write **long ago** or **now** after each one to tell when it happened.

1. The Lopez family came across the ocean on a huge jet airplane. Two hundred other passengers were on the same plane.

   _____

2. Traveling over land by wagon was a long, dusty trip. The roads were all dirt on dry days and all mud on rainy days. The horses' feet kicked dirt up into people's faces.

   _____

3. When the wind stopped blowing, the big sails just hung. The boat drifted slowly. We had to start the engine to get back to the dock before dark.

   _____

4. They had been riding horses a long time when they came to a fence. Most of the horses jumped over the fence, but Joe's horse stopped. Joe was thrown from the horse. Mary stopped a passing truck and asked the people to call a doctor.

   _____

5. Carmen raced down the hill. She leaned too far and fell off her skateboard.

   _____

6. Will wanted to finish reading his book. But he could not since there was not enough light to see the pages. The candles had burned out. Light from the fireplace was very dim. There was no other way of lighting the house at night.

   _____

7. Jane always had to help mother at sunrise. First they lit a fire in the large fireplace in the kitchen. Then they hung a pot of water over the fire to get hot. Then they cooked food in the fireplace most of the day.

   _____

G **Find the right word to use in each sentence.**

crew	appeared	breeze	bonnet
always	darkness	drifted	while
serious	several	stirred	enough

1. At dawn the sun came into sight. Later it went behind a cloud and then _____ again.

2. Just a light wind or _____ would cool us off.

3. What you did is not funny. It is a _____ thing.

4. The wind _____ and moved the leaves a little.

5. Margaret's _____ is tied under her chin.

6. When we walked in the _____, the only light came from the moon and stars in the sky.

7. The boat _____ first one way and then the next as the wind changed.

8. Since _____ of us are going, we will need six lunches.

9. If there is _____, you will have as much as you need.

10. The ship's _____ was made up of the captain and twenty-three sailors.

H **Draw a line from the who or what phrase to each action phrase that makes a good sentence. Make six different sentences.**

Who or What?

1. The sailors

2. A huge wave

3. Some animals

4. The children

Action

a. have fur.

b. work on ships.

c. splashed over the ship.

d. tied their shoes.

e. and passengers.

f. live in the water.

109

Millions of years ago, there were no human beings on earth. There was a time when almost all the world had warm, damp weather. Plants of that time grew very quickly and got very large. The animals also were kinds that we almost never see today on earth, such as dinosaurs and mammoths. Many of those animals disappeared from the earth long before human beings lived here.

If people had been on the earth to see those strange animals and plants, they would have seen one animal then that we see today. It looks the same now as it did a million years ago. Can you guess which animal it is?

Could it be the lion, the strong king of animals? Is it the swift killer, the tiger? Maybe it is the high-flying eagle. No, it is none of these.

It is the turtle. Scientists have tried for years to find out why dinosaurs and mammoths died, while the slow, creeping turtle is still around. Even in this age some turtles may live as long as two hundred years. That is something human beings cannot do. Here are some clues which tell why turtles still live on the earth.

Turtles can live almost anywhere. Some spend their lives swimming in the salt water of oceans. Others live in the fresh water of ponds, streams, brooks, swamps, lakes, and even mud holes. Turtles that are taken from their watery homes and placed on land learn to live in the woods and the tall grass.

Turtles know how to find food easily wherever they happen to live. Ocean turtles eat fish, crabs, clams, shrimp, and snails. Freshwater turtles find tiny fish, snails, insects, water plants, and dead fish. Land turtles eat spiders, roaches, and other insects. They chomp on blueberries, strawberries, mushrooms, worms, and anything else they find.

Turtles have several ways to protect themselves. When in danger, most turtles can pull their heads, tails, and feet into their hard shells. Snapping turtles bite their enemies. Even without teeth, their strong jaws crush and tear. Snapping turtle shells are too small to hide under. Mud turtles never worry about enemies. They smell so bad that other animals will not get close to them.

A **Underline the right answer to each question.**

1. What is the main idea of this story?

   a. Turtles get away from their enemies by crawling into their hard shells.

   b. Turtles have been around for millions of years because they are not afraid of danger.

   c. Turtles have been around for millions of years because they can live well in many different places.

   d. Turtles have been around for millions of years because they eat only good foods.

2. Which of these belong to a turtle?

   a. four feet, two eyes, strong jaws, a mouth

   b. a hard shell, four feet, two eyes, wings

   c. a long neck, two tiny legs, a strong jaw

   d. a mouth, four short legs, a tail, sharp teeth

3. What was most of the world like when dinosaurs lived?

    a. cold and damp

    b. hot and wet

    c. hot and very dry

    d. cold and dry

4. Where would you find a land turtle?

    a. in a large ocean

    b. in a river or a brook

    c. in a swamp or a lake

    d. in a forest or a garden

5. Why are turtles still on the earth?

    a. They crawl very slowly.

    b. They eat very slowly.

    c. They can protect themselves.

    d. They like living here.

6. What do land turtles eat?

    a. berries and bugs

    b. tiny fish and snails

    c. swamps and mud holes

    d. clams and crabs

7. Which lived on the earth first?

    a. human beings

    b. giants and dragons

    c. people

    d. dinosaurs

8. Which of these might see an octopus?

    a. a river turtle

    b. a freshwater turtle

    c. a sea turtle

    d. a land turtle

9. Why do some turtles snap at their enemies?

    a. They have no shells.

    b. Their shells are so large that enemies can crawl in.

    c. Their shells are not large enough to protect them.

    d. They are too lazy to go into their shells.

10. How are some turtles like skunks?

    a. They have thick fur.

    b. They protect themselves with a bad smell.

    c. They have thick shells.

    d. They protect themselves by running quickly.

11. What is fresh water?

    a. water that has not been around long

    b. water that comes from the ocean

    c. water that is not salty

    d. water that is not muddy

12. Which one of these sentences is not true?

    a. Some turtles live for two hundred years.

    b. Turtles are protected by hard shells.

    c. Turtles live in many different places.

    d. Turtles chew food with their teeth.

13. What is the best title for this story?

    a. The People Who Saw Dinosaurs

    b. Millions of Years of Turtles

    c. The Mammoth and the Dinosaur

    d. The Food of the Giant Dinosaur

B **It is hard to remember all the facts you read. Making an outline of the facts will help you remember them. To make an outline:**

1. Write only the main ideas.

2. Put a number or letter by each idea.

3. Use Roman numerals for main ideas:

$1 = I$ $2 = II$ $3 = III$ $4 = IV$ $5 = V$

$6 = VI$ $7 = VII$ $8 = VIII$ $9 = IX$ $10 = X$

Read the facts below. Then make an outline of them.

How Bees Are Like Human Beings

Bees live in groups just as people do. Every bee has a job and must work hard at it. Many bees work together to finish their jobs quickly. Bees that can no longer work are not given food and must die.

Even though bees are fierce fighters, many bees are killed by their enemies. Some ants and bears smash the hives in search of honey. Dragonflies and skunks eat the worker bees as they fly among the flowers. Bees often become ill from a bee sickness and may die from it.

C **The steps to follow to make an outline are given at the left. After you read a step, finish that part of the outline at the right.**

1. Put the title first.

2. Now find the main topic of the first paragraph. Choose one of these:
   a. Live in hives
   b. Live in groups
   c. Die from no food
   Write it next to Roman numeral I.

3. Choose the main topic of the second paragraph. Write it next to Roman numeral II.
   a. Honey makers
   b. Have many friends
   c. Have many enemies

How Bees Are Like Human Beings

I. _____

  A. _____

  B. _____

II. _____

  A. _____

  B. _____

  C. _____

4. Choose some facts from the first paragraph that fit topic I the best. Choose two facts. Write them next to the letters *A* and *B*.
    a. Work together
    b. Work alone
    c. Have their own jobs

5. Choose facts from the second paragraph that fit topic II the best. Write them next to letters *A*, *B*, and *C*.
    a. Butterflies
    b. Skunks
    c. Bears
    d. Sickness
    e. Horses

6. Check your outline. It should look like the one at the right.

How Bees Are Like Human Beings

I. *Live in groups*
    A. *Work together*
    B. *Have their own jobs*

II. *Have many enemies*
    A. *Bears*
    B. *Skunks*
    C. *Sickness*

D **How do these animals protect themselves? Draw lines to match the pictures and sentences.**

1.

2.

    a. It hides inside its shell.

    b. It has a bad smell.

    c. It climbs to treetops.

3.

    d. It has sharp claws.

4.

    e. It hides under water.

5.

    f. It has sharp horns.

6.

    g. It stings its enemies.

E **Now you are ready to outline some main facts from the story on pages 110 and 111.**

1. The title tells you that you will list facts about why turtles have been on the earth for so many years.

2. From these main topics, choose three. Write them next to Roman numerals I, II, and III.

   a. Eat many things
   b. Move very slowly
   c. Live almost anywhere
   d. Protect themselves

3. Here are the facts to prove the topics are true. Write each fact under the right main topic, next to a letter.

   a. Have a bad smell
   b. On land
   c. Dead fish
   d. Insects and berries
   e. In fresh water
   f. Hide in their shells
   g. In salt water
   h. Freshwater plants
   i. Snap at enemies

Why Turtles Have Lived So Long

I. _____

  A. _____

  B. _____

  C. _____

II. _____

  A. _____

  B. _____

  C. _____

III. _____

  A. _____

  B. _____

  C. _____

F **Write the words in the right places with the meanings to play word hopscotch.**

a. crush   b. eagle   c. swift   d. damp
e. snap   f. enemies   g. protect   h. spend
i. million   j. swamps   k. human beings

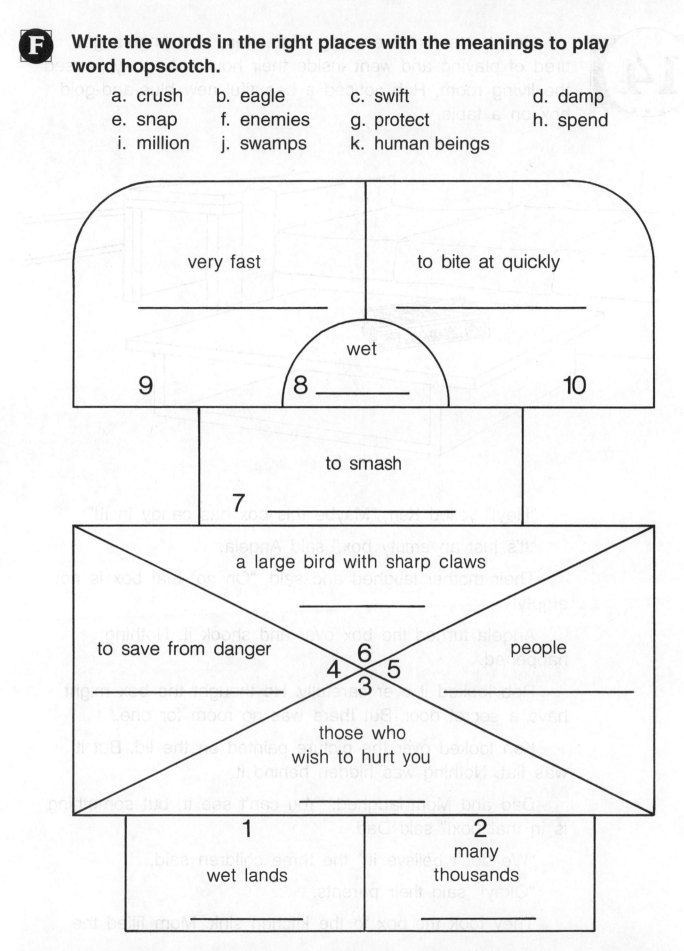

very fast
_____

to bite at quickly
_____

wet
8 _____
9   10

to smash
7 _____

a large bird with sharp claws
_____

to save from danger
_____
4   6
   3   5

people
_____

those who
wish to hurt you
_____

1
wet lands
_____

2
many
thousands
_____

One hot summer evening, Rob, Ken, and Angela got tired of playing and went inside their house. As they passed the living room, Rob noticed a beautiful new blue-and-gold box on a table.

"Hey!" yelled Ken. "Maybe this box has candy in it!"

"It's just an empty box," said Angela.

Their mother laughed and said, "Oh no, that box is not empty!"

Angela turned the box over and shook it. Nothing happened.

Rob looked it over carefully. He thought the box might have a secret door. But there was no room for one.

Ken looked over the picture painted on the lid. But it was flat. Nothing was hidden behind it.

Dad and Mom laughed. "You can't see it, but something is in that box!" said Dad.

"We don't believe it!" the three children said.

"Okay!" said their parents.

They took the box to the kitchen sink. Mom filled the

sink half full of water. Next she took the lid off the box. Then she quickly put the box into the water upside down.

The children were surprised to see little bubbles coming up from around the box. Their mother had to push hard on the box to keep it down. The children took turns holding the box in the water. They too felt the box trying to come up to the top.

Ken's eyes were big with surprise. "What is pushing and making the bubbles?"

"I know!" shouted Rob. "There is something in the box. You can't see it, or smell it, or taste it, but you can feel it. It's all around us and it's in the box, too! It's air!"

"Here is more proof!" said Dad. "Air is in this empty glass."

Dad folded a piece of paper and pushed it into the bottom of the glass. Then he turned the glass upside down into the water in the sink. Again bubbles came up.

Dad had to push hard on the glass to hold it down. Then he pulled it up. When he took the paper out of the wet glass, the paper was dry!

"It must be magic!" whispered Angela.

"No," said Dad. "It's just the air in the glass pushing the water away from the paper."

"I know," said Mom. "Tomorrow let's go to the library and get some books about air. They will show you hundreds of good experiments about air that you can do to surprise your pals."

Underline the right answer to each question.

1. What is the writer of this story trying to tell us?
   a. how to fool our pals
   b. how to surprise our pals
   c. many ways that air helps us
   d. some facts about air

2. What happened last?
   a. The children peeped into the beautiful box.
   b. Dad did an experiment with paper in a glass.
   c. Mom put the box into the water in the sink.
   d. The children got tired of playing.

3. When we <u>experiment</u>, what do we do?
   a. breathe fresh air
   b. always make bubbles
   c. find things in boxes
   d. try things out

4. What happened when Angela shook the box?
   a. Nothing happened.
   b. The lid came off.
   c. It made a loud noise.
   d. Bubbles came out.

5. Why did bubbles form when the glass was put into water?
   a. There was some soap left in the sink.
   b. The paper made bubbles form.
   c. The water was too hot.
   d. Some air got out of the glass and into the water.

120

6. What do we call air that is moving very fast?

    a. a cloud   b. a human being

    c. a wind   d. a living thing

7. Why did Dad have to push down hard on the glass?

    a. The air filled the glass.

    b. He wanted to see if the glass would break.

    c. Dad wanted to break the bubbles.

    d. Dad wanted to know how strong the glass was.

8. Why did Mother say that the box was not empty?

    a. She wanted to tell the children a joke.

    b. She wanted to teach the children.

    c. She made a mistake.

    d. She was telling the children a story.

9. Why is the family going to the library?

    a. for the story hour

    b. to take a walk on a warm day

    c. to find out more about air

    d. to take back some books

10. Why did the paper in the wet glass stay dry?

    a. The air in the glass kept the water out.

    b. The paper in the glass did not let water in.

    c. Dad had put wet paper in the glass.

    d. The bubbles dried the paper.

11. Where do you get your air?

    a. You buy it at the store.

    b. It is everywhere around us.

    c. It comes out of empty boxes.

    d. It comes out of bike tires.

B Air helps to dry things. Air picks up tiny drops of water and carries them away. This is called **evaporation**. Which sentences below tell about water evaporating in the air? Write the word **evaporation** by the ones you pick.

1. _____ After Rita washed the chalkboard, she saw some parts of it dry. As she watched, more dry spots appeared on the wet board.

2. _____ Angela walked through all the rain puddles. Her socks and shoes were getting wet in the water.

3. _____ Rob hung his socks on the line. The next day the socks were dry.

4. _____ After the rain, the flowers were wet and hung down. Soon the water disappeared. The flowers lifted up again.

5. _____ Ted blew into a paper bag. The bag got fatter and fatter. Ted hit the bag. It popped with a loud noise as the air came out.

6. _____ Mom put a pitcher full of iced tea on the table. No one drank any, because everyone was getting ready to go on a trip. Mom forgot to empty the pitcher. The whole family left. No one came into the house while they were on the trip. When they came back eighteen days later, the pitcher of iced tea was half empty.

C Before a fire will burn, it must have air. In a small place, a fire can use up all the air. When the air is gone, the fire goes out because it needs more air. These facts can help you answer the questions below. Circle the right picture and sentence for each question.

1. Robert played with matches. Soon his shirt began to burn. Robert yelled and his whole family ran to help him. What is the best and fastest way to help him?

  a. Give him air.   b. Give him a drink.   c. Cover him.

2. Mr. and Mrs. Gold wanted to burn a huge pile of leaves. They set the leaves on fire. The wind got stronger and blew sparks all around in the air. Mr. and Mrs. Gold were afraid that a house or a tree might catch on fire from the sparks. What is the best and fastest way to stop the fire?

  a. Throw dirt on it.   b. Add more leaves.   c. Run from the fire.

3. The big jet plane made a crash landing at the airport. Quickly the passengers left the plane. But there was still great danger. A fire had started. What is the best and fastest way to stop this kind of fire?

  a. Blow out the flames.   b. Let the wind blow it out.   c. Cover the fire.

D Children at Oaktown School are learning about air. These third graders are going to show the first grade children some easy experiments to teach them about air. Read what each child wants to show. Then read the experiments. Which experiment will prove what each child wants to show? Match them by writing the letter of the experiment next to the child's face.

1. _____

2. _____

3. _____

4. _____

5. _____

Experiments

a. Fill a pan with water. Float a toy sailboat in the water. Blow up a balloon and hold it tightly. Put the balloon opening near the sail. Let the air out slowly. What does the air do to the sailboat?

b. Get a large glass half-filled with soil. Let everyone look at it and touch it. Pour water slowly into the soil. Pour water until it is almost up to the top of the glass. Bubbles will appear. Why?

c. Make a large fan by folding some strong paper. Fan the air close to the children's faces. What will the children feel?

d. Get two large jars with lids. Take off the lids. Put a candle in each jar lid. Carefully light the candles with a match. Carefully place the jar over one of the candles. Turn the jar in the lid several times to make sure the lid is on tightly. Watch the candles. What happens to the two candles? Why?

e. Get a wet rag. Make four wet spots on the chalkboard. Fan the wet spots with your hands or some paper. What happens? Why?

E **Draw lines to match the words and meanings.**

1. good friends	bubble
2. having nothing inside	empty
3. a round body of air	experiment
4. a test to find out about something	believe
5. something we don't tell others about	interesting
6. facts that show something is true	pals
7. so good that we want to know more about it	proof
	secret
8. to put your tongue on something to see what it is	taste

Eddie had lived in a big city all his life. When he was nine, he went to stay all summer with Grandma and Grandpa in the little country village of Oaktown. Eddie was a friendly boy who got to know people easily. Before long, he had many new pals. But sometimes he was unhappy because his friends often teased him. There were many things about the country that Eddie did not know yet. Eddie tried to be a good sport when his pals teased him. But inside he was often hurt and angry.

Grandpa said, "If you don't let them see that you mind, they will soon stop teasing you."

Eddie listened to Grandpa. After a few weeks the other kids got tired of making fun of him. Then they all had many good times together.

One day in August, Eddie was with Bruce and Carol. They were going across a pasture over to the woods. Suddenly they saw something strange.

"Look! A big piece of land has caved in!" shouted Carol. "It did not look like this yesterday."

They looked into a huge hole and saw a tunnel going under the ground.

"There have been several cave-ins around here in the last two years," said Bruce. "My mom and dad made me promise never to go under the earth to explore them."

Carol said, "My parents also told me never to go into the tunnels underground. They made me promise, too! Anyway, I'm sure nothing is down there."

Eddie yelled, "Well, nobody made me promise anything!"

Bruce and Carol helped Eddie down the hole to the beginning of the tunnel.

"What do you see, Eddie?" asked Carol.

There was no answer from Eddie. Carol and Bruce were angry that they could not explore the underground cave.

"Let's fool Eddie," said Carol. "If he finds something down there, let's tell him that it's hens' teeth."

Bruce laughed and said, "No, Carol, let's say turtles' teeth! Even Eddie would not believe that chickens have teeth!"

Inside the cave, Eddie had found some large dirty things that looked like the bones of a huge animal. In the center of the bones was a long stick covered with dirt. The bones and sticks were too heavy to pull out of the cave. Eddie picked up a few shorter sticks and some small round stones to carry out.

"There's something great down there!" shouted Eddie to the others as he came out. "We should tell the newspaper what we found. We are real explorers!"

Carol and Bruce acted as if they were looking at the sticks and stones. They were really trying not to laugh.

When she could keep a straight face, Carol said. "This is an important discovery, Eddie. You have found some turtles' teeth from a huge turtle that lived here millions of years ago. There are no turtles this size living on earth today."

"We should show these to Dr. Grove in town," said Bruce. "She is known all over the world as a scientist. She has discovered bones of animals that lived on earth millions of years ago."

Then the three children ran back through the pasture, over a fence, and down the street to a large green house.

"Eddie, you go in by yourself," said Bruce. "We can't go with you. Dr. Grove might tell our parents that we went underground, too!"

Bruce and Carol hid behind the bushes as Eddie walked up to Dr. Grove's door. Bruce and Carol laughed so hard that they rolled on the ground. Tears ran down their cheeks.

Eddie was scared as he rang the doorbell. A woman came to the door. When Eddie told her about the cave-in, she wanted to know all about it. But when he told her about finding turtles' teeth, she smiled and almost laughed. Eddie began to feel very silly. He had a feeling that his friends might be teasing him again.

But Dr. Grove said, "I would like to see the bigger things you found that you could not carry out. I'll change clothes and we'll go back there together."

Eddie had an idea of how to get even with the others. He said, "Bruce and Carol, my friends, helped me make this discovery. They were the ones who said that these were turtles' teeth."

"Well, let's take them back with us," said Dr. Grove.

All four of them went back to the cave-in. Carol and Bruce told Dr. Grove about the turtle teeth joke and they all laughed. But this joke turned out to be more than just fun.

Dr. Grove found out that the big bones in the cave were part of a giant mammoth from millions of years before. The long dirty stick was a spear thrown by a hunter who had killed the mammoth. Dr. Grove said that scientists had not known before that mammoths and people had lived together at the same time in North America.

The three children's names appeared in the newspaper and on TV for their discovery. In the following years, the names of Carol Jenkins, Bruce Wood, Edward Davis, and Oaktown were in science books for having found proof that the first people who lived in our country were here millions of years ago.

Underline the right answer to each question.

1. What does it mean to try to "keep a straight face"?

    a. to face a straight picture

    b. to keep from laughing

    c. to look straight at someone's face

    d. to draw a picture of a face with straight lines

2. When did Eddie first go down into the tunnel?

    a. the first week he came to Oaktown

    b. before Carol discovered the cave-in

    c. after he went to Dr. Grove's house

    d. after Carol discovered the cave-in

3. Why did Carol say that Eddie had made a big discovery?

    a. She knew that mammoth bones had not been found before.

    b. She was playing a trick on Eddie.

    c. She knew that it is hard to find turtles' teeth.

    d. She wanted to make Eddie happy in the country.

4. What new discovery had the children made?

    a. Mammoths had long fur with stripes.

    b. Early people and mammoths lived at the same time.

    c. The right date of the cave-in was January 29.

    d. Mammoths had dug the large hole in the ground.

5. Eddie was a "good sport." What does this mean?

    a. He was a good ball player.

    b. He got into a tunnel without getting hurt.

    c. His picture was on the sports page of the newspaper.

    d. He tried to get along with others.

6. Why was it funny to tell Eddie that the things he found were turtles' teeth?

    a. Turtles' teeth have points on the ends.

    b. Turtles have no teeth.

    c. They were really hens' teeth.

    d. There were no hens and turtles living long ago.

7. What kind of a doctor was Dr. Grove?

    a. a doctor who takes care of pets

    b. a doctor who takes care of people

    c. a scientist who knows about mammoths

    d. a third grade teacher

8. When was Eddie in Oaktown?

    a. twelve months of the year

    b. June, July, and August

    c. April, May, and June

    d. all of his life

9. How did Grandpa help Eddie make friends?

    a. He yelled at Eddie's pals.

    b. He found the bones.

    c. He caused the cave-in.

    d. He told Eddie not to answer the teasing.

10. What is the best title for this story?

    a. The Discovery of Turtle Teeth

    b. Dr. Grove, the Explorer

    c. A Great Discovery

    d. A Day in the Pasture

B The **main idea** of a story tells what is most important about the story. The title of a story should give you a clue about the main idea. Here are some titles for the story about Eddie, Carol, and Bruce. Which are good titles for the story? Put an **X** by the ones that tell what is important in the story.

_____ 1. The Story of the Cave People

_____ 2. A Great Discovery in Oaktown

_____ 3. Eddie Listens to Grandpa

_____ 4. What Mammoths Looked Like

_____ 5. Exploring Under the Earth

_____ 6. Carol and Bruce Play a Joke

C Many less important facts are in a story to help you understand the main idea. These less important facts are called **details**. Can you give the details about these people? Use the numbers **1, 2, 3,** and **4** for the people's names. One is done for you.

1. Eddie Davis

2. Dr. Joan Grove

3. Carol Jenkins

4. Bruce Wood

___1, 2, 3, 4___ a. lives in North America

_____ b. is a female human being

_____ c. lives in a big city

_____ d. is a child

_____ e. is a male human being

_____ f. is a scientist

_____ g. visits grandparents

_____ h. lives in a village

_____ i. keeps promises to parents

_____ j. works with old bones

_____ k. does not like to be teased

D Scientists have found bones of dead animals that lived millions of years ago. People were not living on earth back then. Scientists have learned enough about these animals to tell what they looked like. Read the details of each discovery. Which scientist worked on it? Write the scientist's name under the picture of the animal he or she studied.

1._____ 2._____ 3._____

4._____ 5._____ 6._____

a. Dr. Morgan found bones of a strange animal in the side of a hill. The animal had been the size of foxes we see today. It had four long, thin legs. It had hard hooves for feet. Dr. Morgan said this animal was a very early kind of horse.

b. Dr. Yee found eggs of strange animals in the rocky earth. These animals were any size from tiny to huge. Their two back feet were claws. Dr. Yee thinks they were very early kinds of birds because on their front claws were large pieces of skin like wings.

c. Dr. Stern studied these strange animals in many parts of the world. These huge animals were covered with thick hair and walked on four thick legs. Dr. Stern thinks they were early elephants because they had long tusks or horns on their faces. They ate grass and other plants.

d. Dr. Garza found teeth of a strange kind of lizard that lived billions of years ago. These large lizards walked on four very short legs. They had long tails that dragged on the ground behind them. They had big pieces of skin and bone on their backs that stood up like huge sails. They killed other lizards for food with their sharp teeth and claws.

e. Dr. Grove became well-known for studying huge lizards that lived near water. They walked on two long, strong back legs. They had short, webbed front feet and were good swimmers. Each had a nose and mouth shaped like a duck's bill.

f. Dr. Serra found the body of this animal frozen in a huge block of ice near the South Pole. This animal looked very much like dinosaurs that ate plants. It had a huge body, a long, thin neck, and a tiny head. But in place of legs it had four flippers. Dr. Serra knew that this animal had lived in the water swimming and eating fish.

E **Draw lines to match the words and meanings.**

1.	something you found	teased
2.	a very tiny town	pasture
3.	made fun of someone	explore
4.	a tool for hunters	yesterday
5.	heard what was said	discovery
6.	the day before today	important
7.	a long hole under the ground	tunnel
8.	to search in strange places	cave-in
9.	said you would do something	spear
10.	a place where the earth sinks	lizard
11.	grassy land where cattle eat	village
12.	an animal that crawls on its four short legs	doorbell
13.	something that rings	listened
		promised

My name is Donna and I'm ten years old. I don't mean to brag, but I am a good detective.

Last autumn my brother Nicky, my parents, and I moved into a large apartment house. Nicky and I have two friends across the hall named Liz and Glenn. In the apartment next door lives a man, Captain Field. He is very friendly to kids and never yells at us. He has collected many interesting things that he shows to us. He even lets us touch them. He often takes Liz, Glenn, Nicky, and me with him when he drives around the city to look for more things to collect.

Glenn once asked, "Did you get all your treasures in this city, Captain?"

"No," answered the captain. "I was in the army. I traveled to many strange places where I found things you never see around here."

One day a man dropped in to see Captain Field.

"Mr. Kimble!" the captain cried out. "What a nice surprise to see you again!"

"I just flew in from Japan," said Mr. Kimble. "I need a place to stay for a few days."

Mr. Kimble stayed with the captain for a week. He was a traveler too and had many interesting stories to tell. My friends and I listened to him for hours at a time.

On the last day of the visit, Mr. Kimble and the captain asked Nicky, Glenn, Liz, and me to come and look at the captain's jewels. It was a stormy day and we could not play outdoors.

The captain kept the jewels in a tiny room that had no windows. The door to that room was always kept locked. The captain unlocked the door and let us in. We were excited to see three glass cases of beautiful jewels.

It was almost time for us to go when the captain said, "Last of all, I want to show you my greatest treasure."

He took out a tiny bag and showed us six large, shining diamonds. Just then the storm outside got stronger. Thunder boomed and all the lights went out! The room became as black as ink.

"Stand still, everybody!" shouted Nicky. "I'll run to the kitchen and get the candles."

The captain said, "I'll feel around for a flashlight."

I stood quietly in one spot because I couldn't see a thing. I heard the others bumping into things as they tried to walk in the darkness. I heard Nicky yell as he ran into a wall while trying to find the door. He kept talking to himself, and I decided to follow his voice.

"I'm in the kitchen because I can feel the sink," Nicky said. I went nearer to his voice. "I found the candles under the sink," Nicky said, "but where are the matches?"

We felt around under the sink. Suddenly I heard a small bang. I knew it was a noise I often heard at home. But in the darkness, I could not remember what made that small bang.

"Who is in the kitchen with Nicky and me?" I called out.

It was very strange that no one answered. But I felt someone brush past me and slip out the door into the hall.

About two minutes later Liz yelled, "The captain found two flashlights!"

Then a beam of light came into the kitchen. The captain and Liz flashed the light on Nicky and me. With this light we found some matches and lit the candles. Each of us had a light as we went back down the hall. Liz went to find Glenn, who had gone into the bedroom by mistake in the dark. The rest of us went back to the treasure room and found Mr. Kimble still sitting there.

"I just can't stand to creep around in the dark," he said.

The captain looked for his diamonds with the flashlight. They were gone!

Just then the lights went on again. The captain searched the whole apartment. We felt terrible because the captain was so upset. I hoped that Liz and Glenn and Mr. Kimble had not stolen the diamonds, because they were all my friends. I knew Nicky and I had not taken them. Though the captain searched us and the apartment, he did not find the diamonds anywhere. We took everything out of our pockets. No one had diamonds on him or her.

"I must think like a detective," I thought. "No one opened the door to leave the apartment while the lights were out. The diamonds must still be here somewhere."

The next day Mr. Kimble was ready to leave. My friends and I came to tell him good-bye. It was not a happy time because everyone was thinking, "Who stole the diamonds?"

The captain was going to drive Mr. Kimble to the airport.

Mr. Kimble said, "I think I'll fix a thermos of cold lemonade to take with me. I'll get some ice cubes now."

He opened the freezer door. Then I remembered! This was the sound I had heard in the kitchen in the dark. I watched Mr. Kimble put the ice cubes into his thermos.

"Just a minute!" I said, even though I was shaking with fear. "Mr. Kimble, I think you should return the captain's diamonds!"

"What do you mean?" snapped Mr. Kimble. "You'd better watch that sharp tongue of yours. It could get you into trouble!"

"Yes, what do you mean?" asked the captain. "Don't speak to Mr. Kimble like that!"

"I heard the freezer door open in the dark last night," I told everyone. "Someone was hiding the diamonds in there because no one took out any food in the dark."

"Are you saying I did it?" asked Mr. Kimble in a cold voice. "Can you prove it?"

Then I really was upset. Could I prove it? I had to think quickly.

"The diamonds are the same color as ice!" I shouted. "The person who stole the diamonds stuck them in an ice cube tray where they would look just like ice."

I took the thermos and carefully put all the ice cubes into a dish. When the ice cubes had melted, six shining diamonds lay in the dish of water!

"They were so beautiful," said Mr. Kimble, "that I just had to have them."

"Donna, I have met many people in my travels, but you are the best detective in the world!" said the captain. "Thank you!"

"It's easy," I said, "because we detectives think!"

Underline the right answer to each question.

1. Why did the children like to visit Captain Field?

    a. He gave them some treasures.

    b. He was their parents' friend.

    c. He was their teacher in school.

    d. He knew how to get along well with children.

2. When did the captain collect most of his treasures?

    a. when he took the children for drives around the city

    b. when he visited his friends

    c. when he traveled with the army

    d. in the autumn

3. What happened just before the lights went out?

    a. The captain unlocked the treasure room.

    b. The children were starting to go home.

    c. The thunder boomed.

    d. The captain said, "I want to show you my diamonds."

4. How did Nicky know that he was in the kitchen?

    a. He felt the sink.

    b. He followed Mr. Kimble in there.

    c. He slipped on an ice cube.

    d. He saw the freezer door.

5. What gave Donna the idea that the diamonds were still in the captain's apartment?

    a. She felt cold when someone passed by her.

    b. Everyone was still in the apartment when the lights came back on.

    c. Nobody but the captain could open the front door.

    d. The doors and windows were kept locked.

6. Who turned out the lights?
    a. Liz and Glen   b. nobody
    c. Captain Field   d. Mr. Kimble

7. What does it mean to have a "sharp tongue"?
    a. The person says clever things.
    b. The person says mean things.
    c. The person gives wrong answers.
    d. The person's tongue has a point on it.

8. Why did Mr. Kimble put the diamonds in ice cube trays?
    a. Diamonds melt if they are not kept cold enough.
    b. The ice cube tray was next to his chair.
    c. The captain never used any ice cubes.
    d. Diamonds are the same color as ice.

9. What happened first after Donna heard a strange noise?
    a. Donna followed Nicky into the kitchen.
    b. Nicky bumped into the sink.
    c. The captain came in with a flashlight.
    d. Someone slipped past Donna and out of the room.

10. How did Donna prove that Mr. Kimble took the diamonds?
    a. She took a picture of him opening the freezer.
    b. She found the diamonds in his pocket.
    c. He was in the treasure room when the lights came on.
    d. She found the diamonds in Mr. Kimble's ice cubes.

11. What is the best title for this story?
    a. Nicky's Lucky Guess
    b. Detectives Must Think
    c. A Visitor Needs Help
    d. Nicky and Donna Move

Draw lines to match these words and meanings.

1. someone who finds missing things   brag

2. a place to live in a large building   autumn

3. important person in the army   apartment

4. to say nice things about yourself   lemonade

5. gathered together in one place   captain

6. a small light to hold in your hand   detective

7. the fall season of the year   collected

8. a hard stone that looks like ice   thermos

9. took something without the right to   stole

10. something that keeps drinks hot or cold   flashlight

11. a large number of people who are ready to fight in times of war   diamond

     jewels

12. things people wear that are made from pretty stones   army

Underline the right answer to each question.

1. Liz and Nicky moved in the autumn. Which is the date that they might have moved?

     a. April 25   b. February 7   c. November 10

2. They moved into a large apartment house. What do we know about where they lived?

     a. Each family had its own large house.

     b. Many families lived in one building.

     c. Several families lived in one room.

3. When there is no light, people cannot see. How might they tell what is around them in the dark?

     a. by hearing, touching, smelling, and tasting

     b. by touching, hearing, looking, and smelling

     c. by smelling, feeling, looking, tasting, and hearing

D A man and a woman stole some jewels. The man hid the jewels in a safe place before the police got him. He would not tell where the jewels are, but he sent a message to the other robber. The message is in code and she is still trying to read it.

A	B	C	D	E	F	G	H	I	J	K	L
2	3	4					9	10			13

M	N	O	P	Q	R	S	T	U	V	W	X	Y	Z
	15					20	21	22		24	25	0	1

1. Can you find out what it says? Finish the code and write the message on the lines. Find the jewels before the robber does.

8-16   21-16   21-9-6   19-6-5   9-16-22-20-6   16-15
6-13-14   20-21-19-6-6-21.   13-16-16-12   22-15-5-6-19
21-9-6   3-10-8   19-16-4-12   10-15   21-9-6   3-2-4-12
0-2-19-5.

_____

_____

_____

2. Circle the place where the robber said to look.

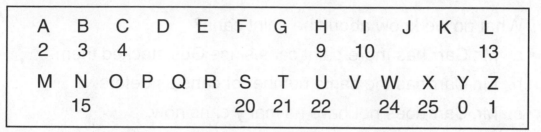

a.   b.   c.

3. In that place is another message in code. What does it say?

11-6-24-6-13-20   2-19-6   10-15   17-10-15-12   7-13-16-24-6-19
17-16-21   16-15   7-19-16-15-21   17-16-19-4-9.

_____

_____

4. Now circle the place where the jewels are hidden.

a.   b.   c.

141

E Can you think like a detective? Read the clues. Then (circle) the right answer.

Mr. Carr had twenty large cans of paint. He asked Gus to stack the cans in four piles. Each pile had to have the same number of cans. Gus finished in a few minutes.

1. What do we know about the paint cans?

   a. Mr. Carr has more paint cans since Gus stacked them.

   b. Mr. Carr has the same number of cans as before.

   c. Mr. Carr does not have as many cans now.

2. How many cans of paint did Gus put in each pile?

   a. four　　b. five　　c. six　　d. seven　　e. eight

Three children were saving money to buy Dad a new wallet for his birthday. Tim had saved four dollars. Tess had saved five dollars. Little John had saved two dollars.

3. Who had saved the most money so far?

   a. Tess　　b. John　　c. Tim

4. Who had saved less money than any of the others?

   a. Tess　　b. Tim　　c. John

5. How much money had the children saved together?

   a. six dollars　　　　b. ten dollars

   c. eleven dollars　　d. twelve dollars

6. The wallet they wanted to buy cost fifteen dollars. What do you know?

   a. They will need more money to buy this wallet.

   b. They will have money left over after they buy it.

   c. They have just enough money to buy it.

7. How much more money will they need to save?

   a. three dollars　　b. two dollars

   c. one dollar　　　　d. four dollars

   e. none

The Oaktown School is different from many other schools. Children there go to school every month of the year. Every month the children get one week off from school.

8. How many months of the year do children go to school in Oaktown?

    a. ten   b. nine   c. twelve   d. eleven   e. twenty

9. How many weeks of the year are the children off from school in Oaktown?

    a. 0   b. 6   c. 10   d. 11   e. 12   f. 20

10. Find out how many days you are off from school this year. Then change the number of days to weeks. Count five school days as a week. What do you know about your school?

    a. You have more time off than children in Oaktown.

    b. You do not have as much time off as children in Oaktown.

    c. You have the same number of weeks off as the children in Oaktown.

    Richard took a small bag of nuts to the park. There were twenty nuts in the bag. He fed eight nuts to a squirrel. He gave nine nuts to a chipmunk. Richard ate the rest of the nuts.

11. What do we know about the bag now?

    a. Now there are some nuts left in it.

    b. Now there are many nuts in it.

    c. Now the bag is empty.

12. How many nuts did Richard feed to the animals?

    a. 0   b. 7   c. 9   d. 17   e. 19

13. How many nuts did Richard eat?

    a. 0   b. 3   c. 5   d. 13   e. 15

14. How many nuts were in the bag when Richard left the park?

    a. 0   b. 2   c. 4   d. 6   e. 8

After you read the story, write the people's names under the houses where they live. Find their names in the story.

Detective Donna Strikes Again

At eleven o'clock, Mother said to Donna, "Will you please go to get your brother Nicky? He has to go to see the doctor at twelve o'clock. He is at Scott's house."

Donna and Mother knew that Scott lived on Dean Road. But they did not know the number of Scott's house. They could not get Scott's phone number, since they did not remember Scott's last name. But Donna was sure she would find the right house.

She went to Dean Street and looked at the five houses.

She knew that the last house must belong to Mary Burns because Nicky had gone to her house before to swim. Donna could tell that the first house was the home of Nicky's friends Jane and Jessie Horn, the best baseball players in the neighborhood.

When she looked at the middle house, she knew that it was the home of Nicky's friend Gus West. Gus always spent Saturday and Sunday working in the large gardens around the house.

Nicky had told Donna that Scott lived next door to Gus. On which side of Gus did Scott live? Donna thought again. She remembered hearing that Mr. Pepper never let children play around the wooden deer in his yard. He always chased children away.

Now Donna knew which house was Scott's. She rang the doorbell and found Nicky and Scott inside.

B **Can you answer these questions about the story? Find each answer at the right. Write it under the question.**

1. Where was Nicky?

   _____

   _____

2. When did Mother tell Donna to go find her brother?

   _____

3. How did Donna find Nicky?

   _____

4. Why did Mother want Nicky?

   _____

   _____

5. How did Donna know that the first house was not Scott's?

   _____

   _____

6. Where was the swimming pool?

   _____

7. Where was the wooden deer?

   _____

8. Who lives in the first house?

   _____

   _____

a. at eleven o'clock

b. to take him to the doctor

c. around the middle house

d. by thinking

e. because of the baseball diamond

f. Mary Burns

g. by using the phone book

h. at a friend's house

i. at twelve o'clock

j. Jane and Jessie Horn

k. at the first house

l. at the fourth house

m. at the last house

This table of contents comes from a book called *Ways of Travel*. Underline the right answers to questions about it.

Table of Contents

1. What do you think this book is about?

    a. different kinds of people

    b. how people get from place to place

    c. how scientists help us travel

2. In which chapter would you read about helicopters?

    a. Chapter 4   b. Chapter 5   c. Chapter 7

3. Which of these might you find in Chapter 6?

    a. a sailboat   b. a coach   c. a jet plane

4. What is the first part of the book about?

    a. how people travel now

    b. how people will travel

    c. how people traveled long ago

5. Which of these might you find in Chapter 4?

    a. travel in a submarine

    b. travel on a sailing ship

    c. travel on a horse

6. What might be found on page 22?

    a. riding on camels and horses

    b. riding on trains

    c. riding in a coach

7. What can we be sure of about this book?

    a. It has only two chapters.

    b. It is about things that are true.

    c. It is about make-believe things.

8. What might be found on page 56?

    a. traveling underground

    b. travel by planes or helicopters

    c. air travel and the cave people

D **What is the topic or main idea of each paragraph below? Look in the Topic Bag. Then write the name of the topic under the paragraph.**

Topic Bag

a. the daytime sky   d. equipment for school
b. how travel began   e. the sky at night
c. the cookbook

All children must bring three pencils to school. They may bring their own paper and a ruler, too.

1. _____

At first, people went places by walking on land. Then they found that they could sit on logs and travel over water, too.

2. _____

Kim picked the book she liked best. It had a picture of food on the cover. Inside were many ways to cook foods.

3. _____

E **Look for the main idea of each paragraph below.**

Wind, Our Friend and Enemy

I.   A strong wind can help human beings. It can quickly dry wet clothes that hang on the line. After rain has fallen, the wind evaporates water that stays on sidewalks and roads. Wind pushes and turns windmills that pump water. Wind pushes against sails of boats and sends them on their way. Wind can be fun for people when it pushes kites and balloons about in the sky.

II.   The strong wind can be bad for human beings, too. It can blow rain and snow into people's faces. Then people cannot see where they are walking. It blows rain and snow about on roads, too. Then drivers may run into things with their cars. Storm winds can blow down trees and signs. Very strong winds even break windows and blow roofs off buildings.

F **Choose the main idea of each paragraph from this box.**

Main Ideas
a. Wind can hurt people.
b. Wind is air that moves fast.
c. People can make air move.
d. Wind can help people.

1. Write the main idea of the first paragraph here.

_____

_____

2. Write the main idea of the second paragraph here.

_____

_____

G **Make an outline of the two paragraphs about the wind. Follow these steps. Use the details in the box below.**

1. First, write the main idea of the first paragraph next to Roman numeral I. Put the main idea of the second paragraph next to Roman numeral II. You wrote the main ideas on page 148.

2. Which details tell more about each main idea? Look in the detail box. Write the details about each main idea next to the letters *A, B, C, D,* and *E.*

The Wind

I. _____

    A. _____

    B. _____

    C. _____

    D. _____

    E. _____

II. _____

    A. _____

    B. _____

    C. _____

    D. _____

    E. _____

Details	
a. Blows rain into faces	f. Dries clothes
b. Helps people have fun	g. Makes driving hard
c. Evaporates water	h. Blows roofs off
d. Makes sailboats go	i. Breaks windows
e. Blows down trees	j. Makes windmills turn

Read the story. Then answer the questions.

Flying High

"My bonnet!" yelled Margaret. She stopped in the middle of the street. Her hands grabbed her head, but the bonnet was gone!

Margaret had left the ribbons on her hat untied. The breeze sailed it down the street. Margaret ran after the hat. The wind was too fast.

A dog ran after it, but he could not reach it. Some men raced for it. But it was too late! The wind changed direction, and the bonnet landed on the roof of a building.

When did these things happen? Write the word **before** or **after** on the line for each phrase.

1. When did the wind change direction?

   _____ the dog ran after the bonnet

2. When did Margaret grab her head?

   _____ the bonnet was gone

3. When had Margaret left the ribbons untied?

   _____ the wind sailed the bonnet away

4. When did men race to get the bonnet?

   _____ the dog ran to get it

5. When did the wind change direction?

   _____ the bonnet landed on the roof

6. Which one fits the end of the story? Circle it.

   The hat fell in the mud.

   A horse stepped on it.

   The hat was in a high place.

   A man put on the hat.

Be a detective and find out where they are. Write the name of the place under each story.

a.

an apartment

b.

a pasture

c.

a library

d.

a tunnel

e.

a jewelry store

f.

a swamp

1. Where is Eddie? He is in a small shop. He sees many cases filled with interesting and shiny jewels. Some of the jewels are diamonds. He is here with his father to buy a shiny gold pin for his mother.

   _____

2. Where is Carol? She is on her parents' farm in a place where grass and weeds are growing. Cows are chewing on the grass. Carol got a drink of water from the brook that runs through this land. There is a strong fence around this place to keep the cows in.

   _____

3. Glen and Nick are exploring deep under the ground. They are in a dark place. They have flashlights to help them see the stones and rocks around them. They can hear the sound of running water from a stream nearby.

   _____

Can you break this code? Fill in the missing numbers. Then write the letters under the numbers to read the message.

A	B	C	D	E	F	G	H	I	J	K	L	M
3	5	7	9		13	15	17		21	23	25	2

N	O	P	Q	R	S	T	U	V	W	X	Y	Z
4		8	10	12	14	16		20	22	24	26	28

16-17-19-14   19-14   16-17-11   11-4-9   6-13   16-17-11
5-6-6-23.

_____

_____

26-6-18   3-12-11   4-6-22   3   5-11-16-16-11-12
12-11-3-9-11-12 !

_____

_____

Use the same code to solve this riddle. Write the letters under the numbers.

1. What do you get when you put ducks in a box?

   3   5-6-24   13-18-25-25   6-13   10-18-3-7-23-11-12-14 !

   _____

2. Now, write your favorite riddle in code.

   _____

   _____

   _____

   _____

Answer Key

Story 1
pages 7–12

A
1. a
2. b
3. b
4. a
5. b
6. c
7. b
8. c

B
1. Ann
2. Mack
3. Mack
4. Joe
5. Kate
6. Kate
7. Beth
8. Ted
9. Joe
10. Sandy
11. Della

C
1. chipmunk
2. whispered
3. resting
4. thinner
5. cheek
6. stripes
7. tired
8. oldest
9. strange

D
1. "said
2. no error
3. the"
4. Oh!"

E
1. "Tomorrow . . . party,"–Joe
2. "I'm . . . birthday." –Mack
3. "I'm . . . now,"/"Come . . . me."
   –Joe
4. no one
5. "This . . . Bob."–Joe
6. "I'll . . . farm,"/"because . . .
   bugs."–Mack
7. "But . . . house," –Joe
8. "Bob . . . things,"/"I'll . . .
   together."–Mack

F
1. Its cheeks were full of seeds.
2. It took the seeds to its home in the ground.
3. It cannot find much food in the winter.
4. It flies south to warmer places.
5. Its mouth was full of seeds.
6. Animals are talking to each other like people do.
7. b
8. b
9. d

Story 2
pages 13–18

A
1. b
2. a
3. b
4. c
5. b
6. c
7. a
8. a

B
2. The Chipmunks' Home
3. New Neighbors Next Door
4. The Man with Five Cats
5. The Spider's Web
6. Worm Pie

C
1. umbrella
2. teacher
3. cover
4. visit
5. otter
6. contents
7. title

D
1. The House Across the Street 12
2. The Day We Bumped into a Skunk 34
3. Teddy Spills the Milk 28
4. The Spider's Web 61
5. Worm Pie 42
6. Jan's Grandmother Comes To Visit 22

E
1. Across the Sea in Sailboats, The Long Walks, How Horses Helped People, Wagon Making
2. Cutting Wood for the Fire, Building a Fireplace, Keeping the Campfire Going
3. Schools in the Old Days, How Children Helped at Home, Children's Games, Toys of the Old Days

F
1. b
2. a
3. b
4. b
5. a
6. b

Story 3
pages 19–24

A
1. b
2. a
3. c
4. b
5. b
6. b
7. b
8. a

B
1. ranger
2. burning
3. stamp
4. camping
5. finish
6. sparks
7. tent
8. careful

C
Make sure the directions for marking the map were followed.

D
1. NS
2. S
3. S
4. NS
5. S
6. NS
7. NS
8. S
9. NS
10. S
11. NS
12. S
13. NS
14. S

E
1. a
2. b
3. a
4. b
5. c
6. c

Story 4
pages 25–30

A
1. c	8. b
2. c	9. a
3. b	10. c
4. a	11. a
5. b	12. a
6. b	13. c
7. c	14. c

B
1. Write "b" in cartoon frame 4.
2. a. to get down to the floor
   b. throw the pie away
   c. Grandmother

C
1. Write "c" in cartoon frame 4.
2. a. A hole was in the roof.
   b. the next time it rains
   c. fix the hole

D
1. skating	4. heavy
2. sled	5. shouted
3. steep	6. mittens

E
1. b	6. c
2. a	7. a
3. c	8. a
4. b	9. c
5. b	10. b

Story 5
pages 31–36

A
1. b	5. c
2. c	6. c
3. a	7. c
4. b	

B
1. eagle
2. c
3. a

C
1. Ralph and Ellen were working on a puzzle.
2. They had worked on the puzzle for two weeks.
3. They went out of the room to ask Mom to look at the puzzle.
4. Mom will help Ralph and Ellen put the puzzle back together.
5. Answers will vary.

D
1. sweeps	2. cleaned
3. club	4. video
5. save	6. cracked

Skills Review
(Stories 1–5)
pages 37–43

A
1. nests
2. farm, rocks, trees, ground
3. a. 39   c. 21   e. 11
   b. 14   d. 41, 54   f. 7
4. c

B
1. Part 4	2. Part 3
3. Part 2	4. Part 3
5. Part 2	6. Part 1

C
1. stripes	4. fire
2. spots	5. white
3. fur	6. safe

D
1. puzzle	6. oldest
2. sparks	7. tent
3. nap	8. ranger
4. title	9. visit
5. stripes	10. shouted

E
1. a	3. c	5. c
2. b	4. c	6. b

F
1. yes	5. yes
2. yes	6. no
3. yes	7. yes
4. no	8. no

G
1. a	3. a
2. c	4. b

H
2. "Good . . . Ralph,"–Detective Sharp Eye
3. no one
4. "You . . . Donna."–Liz
5. "Good . . . think."–Detective Sharp Eye
6. "What . . . Liz?"–Donna
7. "Jack . . . barn."–Donna
8. no one
9. no one
10. "Jack . . . midnight,"–Liz
11. "Good . . . Liz," –Donna

I   1. b   2. d   3. c   4. a

Story 6
pages 44–53

A
1. b	8. d
2. d	9. d
3. b	10. c
4. a	11. c
5. d	12. a
6. a	13. b
7. c	

B
1. equipment	8. boast
2. head	9. ramp
3. champion	10. bones
4. practicing	11. elbow, knee
5. hours	12. busy
6. better	13. stones, hurt
7. awful	14. elbows

C
1. On the Ramp 60
2. What You Must Wear 22
3. Safe Places for Practice 51
4. Tricks on the Skateboard 80

D
1. Styles of Skateboarding 74
2. Safety Tips 31
3. Care of a Skateboard 10
4. Safe Places for Practice 51

E
1. Dictionary
2. Dictionary
3. Table of Contents
4. Dictionary
5. Table of Contents

F   Answers will vary.

G
1. Jenny	6. Jack
2. Julie	7. Alec
3. Erica	8. no one
4. Pam	9. Ed
5. Mom	

Story 7
pages 54–63

A
1. d   4. c
2. a   5. d
3. d   6. b

B
1. relay   5. usually
2. serious   6. muscles
3. praise   7. clumsy
4. relax   8. bounce

C
1. underline *Justin,* circle *can practice*
2. underline *Emily,* circle *shouted*
3. circle *Up, up went,* underline *the baseball*

D Answers will vary.
Examples are
1. at night
2. at eight o'clock
3. during the day

E
1. on the mat
2. on the first floor

F
1. Emily and Justin
   took swimming lessons
   at Woodwell Middle School
   every Thursday and Friday
2. Emily
   learned to dive
   into the pool
   during her second lesson
3. Justin
   does sit-ups
   in his bedroom
   every morning
4. Justin's parents
   took many pictures
   on the playground
   the last day of school

G
1. to see better
2. to have fun
3. to protect her head

H
1. very quietly
2. with her tongue
3. with his car

I
1. in the spring
   many birds
   all over the world
   kill insects
   for food
   In the spring many birds all over the world kill insects for food.
2. every morning
   many children
   travel
   across town
   by car and bus
   to reach the school
   Every morning many children travel across town by car and bus to reach the school.

J
1. to become less clumsy
2. in the water
3. twice a week
4. by doing sit-ups
5. to get better in sports
6. twice a day

Story 8
pages 64–71

A
1. c   7. d
2. b   8. c
3. d   9. d
4. a   10. b
5. c   11. b
6. b   12. d

B
1. brought   6. gobbled
2. capture   7. strange
3. taste   8. beak
4. hooves   9. beautiful
5. protect   10. enemies

C
1. 20   3. 3
2. Most   4. 6

D
1. unlocked   6. unafraid
2. unloved   7. uneaten
3. unanswered   8. unseen
4. unchanged   9. unread
5. unkind

E
1. c   2. b   3. c

F
1. Owls are the greatest mouse and rat hunters in the world.
2. Goats are interesting, funny animals.

G Answers will vary.

Story 9
pages 72–79

A
1. b   7. b
2. d   8. c
3. a   9. c
4. b   10. d
5. d   11. a
6. d

B
1. dam   5. bragged
2. dare   6. scarlet
3. begged   7. anger
4. quills   8. touch

C Write **un** before each word.
1. e   4. d
2. c   5. b
3. a

D
2. The tree shakes a little.
3. The beaver warns the others.
4. Other beavers get out of the way.
5. The beaver takes the last bite.
6. The tree falls.

E
2. after   4. before
3. before   5. after

F
2. g   5. f
3. a   6. b
4. d   7. e

G Check to see that the animals and body parts have been matched correctly.

Story 10
pages 80–87

A
1. a   7. a
2. d   8. c
3. c   9. b
4. b   10. d
5. c   11. c
6. c

B
1. 11
2. Amy, water
3. She was a smart octopus!
4. People came by helicopter from near and far.
5. "That's the smartest octopus in the world!" said all the scientists.
6. They did not know Amy was getting fat from all the food.
7. That was Amy's hardest job.
8. Next, the scientists gave Amy a harder test.

C
1. The octopus finds many foods in the ocean.
2. An octopus is careful when it looks for a home.
3. Other animals are also found in the ocean.
4. The octopus looks very interesting to us.

D Paragraphs will vary. Check to see that sentences support the topic sentence.

E 1st paragraph: People like to eat hot soup in the winter.
2nd paragraph: People eat ham, lettuce, and tomato on their submarine sandwiches. Plants grow on the ocean floor, too.

F
1. camera
2. minute
3. ooze
4. ocean
5. scientists
6. seaweed
7. clever
8. crab
9. tentacles
10. helicopter
11. diet
12. crack
13. clam
14. heavy

Skills Review (Stories 6–10) pages 88–91

A
1. camping
2. ice skating
3. schoolwork
4. baseball
5. diving
6. cooking
7. basketball
8. tennis

B
1. protect
2. plastic
3. praised
4. relaxed
5. enemy
6. brought
7. serious
8. base

C
1. Amy Octopus
2. the beaver's tail
3. The scientists
4. Sam
5. Lita
6. All porcupines

D
1. laughed
2. got broken
3. fell down
4. came faster and faster
5. skated and practiced
6. changed color

E
1. b
2. d
3. a
4. c

F
1. duck
2. frog
3. seal
4. tiger
5. owl
6. bear
7. crab

G Bears have white, brown, or black fur.
Long ago, people used bear skins for rugs.

Story 11 pages 92–101

A
1. b
2. d
3. c
4. a
5. b
6. d
7. a
8. c
9. c
10. d
11. c
12. d
13. a
14. d

B
1. April 3, 1769
2. a. this year's date
   b. 1769
   c. (difference between this year and 1769)
3. a. (difference between this year and 1869)
   b. 100

C
1. engine
2. passengers
3. captain
4. trunk
5. traveling
6. mainsail
7. fin
8. crowded
9. shark
10. parents
11. always

D
1. a
2. b
3. c
4. b
5. c
6. b
7. b
8. b
9. a. Margaret Scott
   b. John Scott
   c. 12

E
1. who or what
2. the action
3. phrases

F

	Underline	Circle
1.	Fish	can swim
2.	The wind	blew harder
3.	The ship	is turning
4.	Sam	fell down
5.	Margaret	ran quickly
6.	A sailor	pulled hard

G Write an **S** by sentences 2, 3, 6, and 7.

H
1. before
2. before
3. after
4. before
5. before
6. after

I
1. c
2. d
3. b
4. a

J Paragraphs will vary.

Story 12 pages 102–109

A
1. d
2. d
3. a
4. b
5. a
6. d
7. d
8. b
9. c
10. b
11. a
12. d

B
1. 21
2. 3
3. 4
4. 70
5. a. Columbus's
   b. 277

C
1. morning, dawn, noon, sunrise
2. bedtime, evening, darkness, midnight

D
1. h   5. f
2. d   6. c
3. e   7. a
4. b   8. g

E
1. c   4. d
2. a   5. b
3. b   6. c

F
1. now   5. now
2. long ago   6. long ago
3. now   7. long ago
4. now

G
1. appeared   6. darkness
2. breeze   7. drifted
3. serious   8. several
4. stirred   9. enough
5. bonnet   10. crew

H
1. b, d   3. a, f
2. c   4. d

Story 13
pages 110–117

A
1. c   8. c
2. a   9. c
3. b   10. b
4. d   11. c
5. c   12. d
6. a   13. b
7. d

B Outlines may vary.

C Completed outline should read:
How Bees Are Like Human Beings
  I. Live in groups
    A. Work together
    B. Have their own jobs
  II. Have many enemies
    A. Skunks
    B. Bears
    C. Sickness

D
1. d   2. g
3. f   4. b
5. c   6. e

E Completed outline should read:
Why Turtles Have Lived So Long
  I. Eat many things
    A. Dead fish
    B. Insects and berries
    C. Freshwater plants
  II. Live almost anywhere
    A. On land
    B. In fresh water
    C. In salt water
  III. Protect themselves
    A. Have a bad smell
    B. Hide in their shells
    C. Snap at enemies

F
1. swamps   6. eagle
2. million   7. crush
3. enemies   8. damp
4. protect   9. swift
5. human beings   10. snap

Story 14
pages 118–125

A
1. d   7. a
2. b   8. b
3. d   9. c
4. a   10. a
5. d   11. b
6. c

B Write *evaporation* beside sentences 1, 3, 4, and 6.

C
1. c   2. a   3. c

D
1. b, c   4. d
2. e   5. c, b
3. a

E
1. pals   5. secret
2. empty   6. proof
3. bubble   7. interesting
4. experiment   8. taste

Story 15
pages 126–133

A
1. b   6. b
2. d   7. c
3. b   8. b
4. b   9. d
5. d   10. c

B Mark an X by sentences 2, 5, and 6.

C
b. 2, 3   g. 1
c. 1   h. 2, 3, 4
d. 1, 3, 4   i. 3, 4
e. 1, 4   j. 2
f. 2   k. 1

D
1. Dr. Garza
2. Dr. Stern
3. Dr. Serra
4. Dr. Morgan
5. Dr. Grove
6. Dr. Yee

E
1. discovery   8. explore
2. village   9. promised
3. teased   10. cave-in
4. spear   11. pasture
5. listened   12. lizard
6. yesterday   13. doorbell
7. tunnel

Story 16
pages 134–143

A
1. d   7. b
2. c   8. d
3. c   9. d
4. a   10. d
5. b   11. b
6. b

B
1. detective   7. autumn
2. apartment   8. diamond
3. captain   9. stole
4. brag   10. thermos
5. collected   11. army
6. flashlight   12. jewels

C
1. c   2. b   3. a

D
1. Go to the red house on Elm Street.
Look under the big rock in the back yard.
2. b
3. Jewels are in pink flower pot on front porch.
4. a

E
1. b   8. c
2. b   9. e
3. a   10. Answers will vary.
4. c   11. c
5. c   12. d
6. a   13. b
7. d   14. a

Skills Review (Stories 11–16) pages 144–152

A
(1st) Jane and Jessie Horn
(2nd) Scott
(3rd) Gus West
(4th) Mr. Pepper
(5th) Mary Burns

B
1. at a friend's house
2. at eleven o'clock
3. by thinking
4. to take him to the doctor
5. because of the baseball diamond
6. at the last house
7. at the fourth house
8. Jane and Jessie Horn

C
1. b   5. c
2. c   6. c
3. a   7. b
4. c   8. b

D
1. equipment for school
2. how travel began
3. the cookbook

E No responses

F
1. Wind can help people.
2. Wind can hurt people.

G Completed outline should read:
  I. Wind can help people.
    A. Helps people have fun
    B. Evaporates water
    C. Makes sailboats go
    D. Dries clothes
    E. Makes windmills turn
  II. Wind can hurt people.
    A. Blows rain into faces
    B. Blows down trees
    C. Makes driving hard
    D. Blows roofs off
    E. Breaks windows

H
1. after
2. after
3. before
4. after
5. before
6. The hat was in a high place.

I
1. a jewelry store
2. a pasture
3. a tunnel

J This is the end of the book. You are now a better reader!

K
1. A box full of quackers!
2. Answers will vary.

158